ROMANS PROVES PAUL LIED

HAVE WE INHERITED LIES FROM OUR FATHERS?

RICHARD EPLER

Author's Tranquility Press
ATLANTA, GEORGIA

Copyright © 2024 by Richard Epler

All rights reserved. No part of this publication may be reproduced, distributed or transmitted in any form or by any means, including photocopying, recording, or other electronic or mechanical methods, without the prior written permission of the publisher, except in the case of brief quotations embodied in critical reviews and certain other noncommercial uses permitted by copyright law. For permission requests, write to the publisher, addressed "Attention: Permissions Coordinator," at the address below.

Richard Epler/Author's Tranquility Press
3900 N Commerce Dr. Suite 300 #1255
Atlanta, GA 30344
www.authorstranquilitypress.com

Ordering Information:
Quantity sales. Special discounts are available on quantity purchases by corporations, associations, and others. For details, contact the "Special Sales Department" at the address above.

Romans Proves Paud Lied-Have We Inherited Lies From Our Fathers?/Richard Epler
Paperback: 978-1-964362-82-3
eBook: 978-1-964037-79-0

INTRODUCTION

Personal background

First things first – I make no claim to represent any Church, or to be a world class Bible scholar with Doctorates in Semitic Scriptures, Greek, or to have participated in Biblical Archeology or studies into ancient Middle or Near East history. Aptitude tests taken in High School did score well for abstract thinking ability… which has been very useful to observe patterns of evidence throughout my studies. For years I've been reading extensively from the best scholars available about the differences between Christian and Jewish translations of the Scriptures, the records from the Dead Sea Scrolls, scholarship to see if what we have has been altered – or not, contradictions, inconsistencies, and if what the Bible says really happened, was it telling events that match what archeology has found in the ground, or from historical records of other nations contemporary with ancient Israel – or not? I am completely indebted to the work of others that have each provided needful information and evidence to find answers to many questions I had. I cannot say any of the scholars support my findings, but I cannot honestly say the weight of the evidence supports a different conclusion.

What I'm telling is my opinion of where the facts led me to conclude. You may decide I'm wrong – but given the seriousness of my discoveries – I hope you will at least consider the evidence so you can decide where you choose to reside. You will not hear these things at Church or a Seminary because there is an existing gulf between top level scholars who deal with fact-based evidence, as opposed to those who are busy learning how to best present a case to believe the status-quo doctrines of any particular Church. It's a significant issue, and students from Seminary education are generally those who have the deep desire to learn more, as I have also had, to then take on the issue of the reliability of our Scriptures, ancient languages, histories, etc.. I've heard that at least half the Doctorate level graduates do not go on to vocations as Ministers/Preachers. There is a gulf that should not exist if people at all levels were more open minded to consider if our record of Scriptures has been altered over a long period of time. At the end are noted some of the books I've read - for your consideration.

I will confess to having been a fervent supporter of Paul most of my life, as that is what I was indoctrinated to do by my parents, siblings, and Church. I'm third generation of Church of Christ preachers, my father and grandfather were both ministers. Born in a little burg in Ohio (Fresno), when I was four our dad decided to go from being a butcher to a preacher and moved our family of seven to Utah to convert the Mormons. ("Work not for the meat which perishes")

Thereafter, for as long as I can remember, living at home centered on quoting the Bible as often as possible and attending every service and Bible class. I considered preaching as my dad and two brothers before me, did a bit over a year at David Lipscomb as a Bible major and Sociology minor, but it just didn't feel right for me. I felt no draw to be preaching to those who were much older and wiser than I was and was scolded by one of the Elders after my first sermon, about faith, and was told to never preach like that in his church again. I'd witnessed the trials my dad had to keep his preaching jobs, and we usually moved every couple of years, which afforded me the good experience of having grown up from New Jersey to California. God said to honor our parents, but there comes a time in life when we mature enough to realize we have to independently be responsible to God, as one of His Standards is of individual accountability – if our parents were wrong about something – or we are convinced by the Teachings of God that we need change in our pathway to be on His path – we will not be justified to tell God we had to ignore Him so we could do as our earthly father told us to live or believe.

If God has spoken, that is who every one of those who believe in God or Jesus should repent to believe. The best telling of this principle is in Ezekiel 18, and Jesus taught likewise in Matthew. Each is responsible for their own actions, whether good or evil. Also, the good of a righteous person cannot be counted to an evil person, and the evil persons evils cannot be ascribed to a righteous person – each is personally accountable to God. If a righteous person, then turns and does evil – their righteousness before will not be accounted to them, and likewise, the evil person, if they turn to do all that Elohim declared righteous and good and forsake their evil – their former evil will not be accounted towards them.

Where in Matthew did Jesus teach his blood was a sin sacrifice, or that his righteousness would be accounted to anyone but himself? Where does Christianity get the idea that they are saved by the blood of Jesus – that God offered up His only Son as a sacrifice to forgive His enemies, or anyone else? Where does Christianity get the idea that eating the body or blood of Jesus – whether by proxy symbolism or belief the Holy Spirit performs transubstantiation to it, so it literally is his body and blood – how on earth does this differ in substance from those Christians deemed savages for being cannibals? Jesus taught nothing of magic wine or crackers. Jesus taught the need to repent and serve God alone, and that love for your fellow is in partnership to the Greatest Commandment, that love is the peg the Law hangs upon – love of God and love for our fellow human being.

All I knew about was Church, the rest of the congregation had to work and live in the secular world, of which I was ignorant because of my upbringing – what should I presume to tell them?! The most useful information from my dad was "Keep your nose clean" – with no useful info or antidotes. I suspect this was because he was never successful in keeping jobs – before, and during his preaching career, if one could call it that. Due to my unjust reliance on Paul's writings, I thought he was brilliant – as his teaching, I later observed, were little but circular reasoning, myth, straw-men, and contradictions against what Jesus was really teaching – had I just been taught to grasp the harmony of Jesus' teachings to the Covenant Standards given by Elohim – life would have been lived better and made more sense. It is my intent to share what I've learned with you, the reader, as no Church or Bible publisher is going to tell you these things that have been learned at great personal cost – but are shared here openly.

I was perhaps the most faithful student of Paul for most of my life. I'd read the gospels, wondered at the differences, was taught to draw a veil over my mind to pretend Paul was making sense of the gospel for "us" gentiles, who knew little of the Jewish religion of Judaism. It was later in life, when realizing Paul could not have been teaching the same as Jesus, that I read the most difficult book of my entire life: "Jesus Words Only", by Douglas DelTondo, upon recommendation from a fellow poster at an LDS/Evangelical debate site. My two brothers who were preachers, neither my dad, were able to offer any answers to the points made in the book. I even bought a copy of the book for one of my brothers, but he didn't read it and the next thing he did was stop communicating with me and call me a heretic for not believing Paul. My oldest brother kept some correspondence over time, but never answered any of the points of question. Later he finally admitted there was no Scriptural basis for "the lamb of God" comment in the gospel of John, and ending with his telling me all my mail was going to be placed in his "Spam" folder.

When I wrote "One Disciple to Another, the Original Jesus," largely centering on Jesus' teachings in the Sermon on the Mount, the elders at my church said they would read it and we could discuss any issue they might have before I thought to share the book with the members. Much to my surprise, they stopped me at the door of the church to tell me they were doing a special Elders presentation to tell everyone not to read the book – breaking their agreement that we would get together and discuss anything they wished to.

I've had like experience with every other Church – people were interested, but their leadership squashed the book. I find this extremely odd because the book was mainly about the gospel as taught by Jesus in Matthew, and that we do as Jesus commissioned – that we learn from them about what Jesus taught – to be disciples of Jesus. Therefore, I have no doubt if Jesus were to show up in any Church today and preach what he did in Matthew – he would quickly be given the "left foot of fellowship" by all the Churches leadership.

Background on the book of Romans:

Romans was not considered New Testament Scripture for the first three centuries by the original disciples of Jesus (Joshua). The Protestant Reformation was started by Martin Luther and John Calvin – both of which relied heavily on the writings of Paul, especially Romans. Romans is the best book from Paul to grasp understanding of his gospel, just as Matthew is the best book to understand the gospel taught by Jesus.

The New Testament Canon Chart shows all the early church was composed of the disciples of Jesus, three sects, and all were unanimous to reject every writing of Paul. The first three centuries of their history included battling what they considered to be lies against the gospel of Jesus, that Paul taught to negate the Law (Covenant), which Jesus taught was necessary. Practically all early evidence was destroyed by Rome because they promoted the writings of Paul, as without his words most of what we consider "Christianity" would not have survived beyond his lifetime. Much of the ancient view of Paul was gleaned from writings found with the Dead Sea Scrolls and was documented by Robert Eisenman. Jesuswordsonly.org contains many references to his work.

Paul's usefulness to Rome was his gospel being morphed to be more like beliefs in Mithraism – the god of the Roman soldiers. Books have been written about the similarities, so if you want to read up on that – this is not going to be a source for that. What will be exposed herein is comparing Paul's writings to the teachings of Jesus in **Matthew and the records of the Hebrew Scriptures – the** most ancient accounts. I say the most ancient accounts because we all have records that have been altered by Judaism and by Romanism. Judaism largely began about 444 - 260 BC, with the pact signed in Nehemiah [10]; and thereafter the Persian commission to translate the writings of Moses, the Law, into Greek. Modern scholarship gives good reason to think this is when Judaism began, by the Persians paying to have their "Law" in Greek – and many evidence show in all the history of Israel it was not as told in current translations of the Hebrew or Greek. See "The Origin of Judaism", and the chapter titled "Conclusions."

Roman Church authority dates at least as early as the Council of Nicaea 325 AD. "Catholic" means "universal" church – one roof to cover over many of the divisions that were taking place by then – largely due to invented gospels and people like Paul who never met Jesus but told their own stories or secondhand testimony about Jesus. This was not an effort to restore the faith taught by Jesus, this was a political effort to place Roman authority over the "Church Universal" and thereafter to persecute or kill those who did not submit to the Roman Church rule – which went on for over 1000 years. Had I been alive back then, there is no doubt Rome would have killed me for writing about these things or providing evidence they have been rejecting the true accounts of Jesus and God from their inception.

I make these claims upon this primary evidence:

1. The gospel of Matthew, especially the unromanized Hebrew Matthew of Shem-Tob, as likely copied from a Jewish record for a debate and was re discovered and translated by George Howard. Evidence shows it is altered, but not Romanized as much as our Greek based Matthew. This is the closest I've found available today for the teachings of Jesus (Joshua) that was the sole record of authority for over 200 years after Jesus. The next best account is the Matthew in the "Aramaic English

New Testament" by Andrew Roth. Paul was of little concern since everyone abandoned following him in his own lifetime – see 2 Timothy 4:19 – no one continued to believe or follow Paul thereafter? Those were his words – not mine! Records have been found that he was noted as a liar. That is a different study that others have well documented, such as Douglas DelTondo, in "Jesus Words' Only." My focus is on Matthew's record because that is the one book of authority in the first two centuries for the followers of Jesus. It was written like a textbook to know what Jesus had taught his disciples, which was to inform all future disciples by their firsthand testimony of him.

2. The records of the Covenant match the teachings of Jesus. This was noted before translations of the Shapira scrolls came out in 2021, mainly in "The Valediction of Moses" (V) by Idan Dershowitz. I have been digesting my observations in "V" and the gospel of Matthew for a few years now, and to sum it up: Jesus was teaching the Standards given by God in the original Sinai Covenant as no other prophet in the history of Israel! Jesus was "putting legs" to the words of God. I believe this is why the teachings of Jesus have drawn so much admiration for thousands of years – and the teachings of Jesus reflect the Covenant Standards of God so closely that we would have to be blinded to not see their alignments. From my perspective, this is modern proof that what Jesus taught was directly inspired by Elohim! Jesus taught the truth – and it was Judaism who had altered the Covenant Words of God about 1000 years before him!

3. Those of Elohim – the Father in heaven – must use His Instructions to determine who He said we must hear, and who He said we must ignore. Isaiah summed it up as "If they speak not according to the Law and the Testimony, there is no light in them." God summed it up in our records of Deuteronomy 4, 12, 13 and 18.

4. If someone works miracles, and/or gives true prophecy – if they teach a different god, or if they teach against His Sabbath, or they teach against any of the Decrees, Blessings, or Curses – Elohim said we must ignore them. Most everyone is deceived by altered scriptures, most everyone of strong belief or faith has relied heavily upon false testimony, to the point of rejecting the spoken and written words of Elohim, the prophets, and That Prophet – Jesus. This is written with the intent to free all mankind from lies taught in the name of God – be they from Paul or Jewish Rabbinical lore. Don't be ashamed for not having realized we've been lied to – God forgives when we repent to do His will indeed. The curse is to falsely testify in His name – and He desires no one perish. (Ezekiel 18)

5. Jesus taught to dig down to the bedrock to build your house upon it, so the storms would not cause it to fall. The storms are here. Anchor yourself to the Rock! When

you understand Jesus, you will also know God as never before, and you will gain an entirely new appreciation and understanding from the Psalms. There is complete harmony between the words of God, the teachings of Jesus, the Psalms and the Prophets. This is primary proof Rome and Judaism gave us bad records. **In the Romans review comments you may note differing names for Jesus – Yeshua, Y'shua, Yehoshua, Joshua, or Joshua 2.**

Questioning Paul was a hot topic in the first centuries of the Church, before Rome hijacked the Christian faith. Our current scriptures provided adequate evidence that Paul was nothing but a liar, or a severely delusional man - take your pick. The words of Paul's own mouth condemn him! Most Christian scholars have not tried to be reasonable to explain Paul's contradictions of doctrine or facts of his conversion, or that his teachings also defied the everlasting Covenant and the teachings of Jesus.

We need to open our ears and stop putting blinders over our eyes - LOOK at Paul in his own testimony!

Who was the real Paul? For starters, he claimed to be a Jew of the tribe of Benjamin - Jew of Jews, a pinnacle of virtue of the Law, understanding the depths of many things. Well, that my dear friends is a lie, as all his writings are filled with lies. Robert Eisenman, one of the best scholars of record regarding ancient Christian and DSS writings did an article identifying Paul was a Herodian. In case you didn't recall off-hand, this is the family of the man who ordered killing the infants in Bethlehem near the time of Jesus' birth.

Robert Eisenman: "Paul as Herodian" (drew.edu)

The King James Version of the Bible is much revised over 400 years, so I wanted to use the NIV. Copyright conditions for the NIV prevent using an entire book of the NIV. I also doubt any Bible publisher would condone what is being told in these writings, as they do not find accord to the Nicene Creed. Problems with the writings of Paul can easily be exposed in any translation – because they are based upon the same base textual evidence. The KJV text will be noted for review and comments for most of this review, to ensure less than 50% of the NIV is used. I don't want to burst the bubbles of the KJV only crowd, but he was a very wicked man. Read the book he wrote just before commissioning his authorized Bible version: "Demonology." You should read up on who you've trusted your soul to – and I cannot imagine that Bible publishers have never been aware of his previous book…

Comments will be inserted below the text throughout Romans, but in a **bold font**, so as to avoid confusion and enable comment throughout the book of Romans. To my knowledge no one has taken this on before, but I'll be doing my best to pass on what I've been able to understand at this point of my life (71).

King James Version

Romans 1

¹ Paul, a servant of Jesus Christ, called to be an apostle, separated unto the gospel of God,

[Paul first claims to be a "servant" of Jesus. Was Paul a faithful servant, or a wicked servant? Recall Jesus' parables about servants. Judge righteously, was Paul faithful, or not? How could he have been faithful if he taught against doing what his "Lord" said his disciples will do? Jesus is recorded to have said; "Why do you call me "lord" and not do as I say?" The only record Paul was "called to be an apostle" is from his own writings. Where does Acts claim Paul was an apostle? His first account doesn't make this claim at all. It isn't until Acts 22:21 that we hear Paul's claim that Jesus said "Depart, for I will send you far from here to the Gentiles." This latter claim, given under oath, totally defies what was recorded earlier in Acts – to go to a specific disciple and he would be told what he must do. There is no witness testimony to this "apostle" claim but Paul's words to Luke. (Luke and Acts were written by the same person and are secondhand testimony until later in Acts.) The most important evidence about Paul will stem from the Instructions of God and Jesus to see if Paul remains faithful to the Teachings of God in the Covenant Standards and the teachings of Jesus. As Isaiah said, "If they speak not according to the Law and the Testimony, there is no light in them."]

² (Which he had promised afore by his prophets in the holy scriptures,)³ Concerning his Son Jesus Christ our Lord, which was made of the seed of David according to the flesh;⁴ And declared to be the Son of God with power, according to the spirit of holiness, by the resurrection from the dead:

[Note that the internet source provides no footnotes scriptural support for the claims of Paul in verses 2 and 3 prophecy for "his earthly life" or that Jesus claimed to be "the Son of God in power by his resurrection from the dead" In fact, the claim of Jesus in Matthew is to be a mortal man – not a pre-existent "Son of God" – which In other writings Paul also claims to be "co-Creator of the heavens and earth." In Matthew, Jesus was "begotten" by God at his baptism, not his birth in Bethlehem. Israel was declared by God to be His son, and Jesus was the unique one, the one anointed by God to speak on His behalf in calling all men to repent and turn from iniquity (lawlessness - because they had altered His Covenant 1000 years before, and Israel was following their Rabbi instead of

the Teachings of Elohim). See Jesus' claim during his trial near the end of Matthew to be the one who would ascend to the throne on the right hand of God – as foretold in Daniel. The false charge was Jesus claimed to be "the Son of God" to be blasphemy because there is only One God – see the Covenant and Isaiah 43-45.]

5 By whom we have received grace and apostleship, for obedience to the faith among all nations, for his name: 6 Among whom are ye also the called of Jesus Christ:

NIV: 5 Through him we received grace and apostleship to call all the Gentiles to the obedience that comes from[c] faith for his name's sake. 6 And you also are among those Gentiles who are called to belong to Jesus Christ.

[God said everything – all - including mankind – belong to Him, not Jesus. God is our creator and source of being and mankind was created in His image with specific purpose in His creation of the heavens and earth. Jesus called all men to repent and obey God. Proof texts given in the Sermon on the mount and the rest of his teachings prove they are founded upon, and in total accord with, the words of God in the Covenant. In Matthew the charge of Jesus was to make disciples of him from all nations – not just Jews. The twelve apostles were already making disciples – so Jesus had no need to send Paul to do what they were already doing. None of the chosen apostles of Jesus ever said Paul was an apostle – only Paul's personal biographer Luke ever implied such (by writing Acts of the Apostles and making Paul the main character) – and he never directly said Paul was one of the apostles of Jesus. The main point is Jesus taught according to the Covenant – that God has grace towards those who abandon evil and learn to improve themselves by observing and doing the Standards given by Elohim, and finds total alignment to both Isaiah 1 calling us "Come, let us reason together" so that we would understand and turn to Him to do what He said is good – to live uprightly before Him and our fellow mankind, and this is when, even though our sins be as crimson, they will become white as snow. The Standard is to do no evil and to grow in doing what is blessed. Those are about observing and doing the stated will of God – not about "obedience that comes from faith for his name's sake". Pretending it is about "faith" and "for his name's sake" are just muddying the mind of the hearer so they will start thinking like Paul, rather than Jesus and his apostles. With God there is no mystery, because it is about knowing and observing what we do, not what we "believe" or "faith" to be true.]

7 To all that be in Rome, beloved of God, called to be saints: Grace to you and peace from God our Father, and the Lord Jesus Christ.

[It was Rome who gave authority to the Catholic Church, who put Paul into our New Testament records – and persecuted everyone who would not believe the lies of Paul and the Pope. The murders and persecutions from Rome find no accord with anything Jesus taught or exampled. If Paul found favor with Rome, it is because he was related to the Roman Herodian family (recall the king who had all the children at Bethlehem killed? – which is documented at: Jesuswordsonly.org and by Robert Eisenman). One only needs to read the Ten Commandments in the Hebrew translation to know those God has grace and peace towards are those who love Him and observe His Commandments to be their manner of life. God also said those who have His Commandments and reject His Covenant Standards are His enemies – said to unfaithful Israel – not those they lied to. Did Paul teach upholding the least of the Commandments of God as Jesus did? In some places Paul seems to, but then in other places he defies the good he did say. If you believe Paul - you only show you have not judged Paul by God given Standards. No wonder Paul said he caught some by his guile, and in another place that he strove to be all things to all men - to the Jews as a Jew, to the Gentiles, as a Gentile. The Standards of Elohim Almighty defy this and condemn all forms of deceit and false testimony.]

Paul's Longing to Visit Rome

[8] First, I thank my God through Jesus Christ for you all, that your faith is spoken of throughout the whole world. [9] For God is my witness, whom I serve with my spirit in the gospel of his Son, that without ceasing I make mention of you always in my prayers; [10] Making request, if by any means now at length I might have a prosperous journey by the will of God to come unto you.

[Paul, or any other imaginator, can say they are following "my spirit", but we also test "spirits" and "minds" by the same Instructions from God to know if someone is to be believed or not! Surely, we can judge all by the word of God – that is what He told us to do! We cannot know the "spirit" or "mind" of Paul aside from evidence of what he left us all in his writings. Paul could not have been serving as a messenger of God unless he was upholding every Standard given by God – never defying His instructions, Covenants, Commandments, or standards of justice and judging righteously. Is the message from Paul's preaching and writing the same as what Elohim gave, as the record of Jesus' disciples in Matthew? Paul says that his spirit is known by his preaching – "whom I serve in my spirit in preaching the gospel". Since he said he was preaching "the gospel of his Son – how can we know if Paul did except, we first compare the teachings of Paul to the teachings of Jesus, after all, Jesus was preaching the gospel of the Kingdom of God, and we have a good record of that in Matthew. Do Paul's teachings find accord to the teachings of Jesus in Matthew? If Paul taught the gospel of Jesus – "his Son" – there would be as much accord in Paul's letters to Matthew as Matthew has to the 3000-year-old Law/Covenant and the Prophets. It should be extremely easy to observe if he did or not. I've checked it out, and invite every living person on the planet earth to do what I did to see for themselves that Paul absolutely lied when he made this vital statement of fact. Don't just imagine or pretend or believe Paul without having ensured the matter is so, or not – check the facts so YOU WILL KNOW! As for Paul coming to Rome – he came in chains and reportedly died there due to his incident at the Temple vows in Acts, and I no longer believe the claims of Paul, Peter, or Steven in Acts either – because Acts was evidently written to cause us to think Paul was a true apostle of Jesus – when he probably was not. In his letters, Paul certainly taught the middle wall of separation in the Temple was done away with (demarcation between area for Gentile prayers from the Jewish section) – Paul's disciples defiled the Temple because they believed Paul and disbelieved the word of God? Do your own evaluation of Paul - don't trust those 'faithful Bereans' who didn't have any of his writings. Open your eyes wide for this one. Paul reveals his "spirit" in Romans 7:24-25, King James Version

[24] ["O wretched man that I am! who shall deliver me from the body of this death? [25] I thank God through Jesus Christ our Lord. So then with the mind I myself serve the law of God; but with the flesh the law of sin."] According to Paul, our flesh is where sin proceeds from. Even though we sin, in our spirit we serve God, even though we are sinning! Try to find anywhere Elohim or Jesus said this!! If we believe Paul, our understanding and conscience must be placed above what God decreed from the beginning. Paul taught that whatsoever we think is a sin is then a sin to us - even when Elohim said no such thing. Paul said lowly angels gave the Law as a curse to Israel, but God declared it was to bless everyone who will live by His Instructions and help us live life as He said it should be. Elohim told Cain, "Surely if you improve yourself, you will be forgiven", and therefore all of us should have had that record, if our Bible publishers had interest to help us understand His will and ways and know that Elohim is our Redeemer and Savior. (Isaiah 43 - 47) Perhaps the greatest evil Paul taught was to say we are not responsible for our sins because we are made of flesh - we can't help it - which is absolutely against everything God, the Prophets and Jesus taught about sin.

[11] For I long to see you, that I may impart unto you some spiritual gift, to the end ye may be established; [12] That is, that I may be comforted together with you by the mutual faith both of you and me. [13] Now I would not have you ignorant, brethren, that oftentimes I

purposed to come unto you, (but was let hitherto,) that I might have some fruit among you also, even as among other Gentiles.

[What "spiritual gift" is Paul known for imparting to anyone? What "gift" does anyone receive from Paul today, except to disbelieve the Teachings and Standards given by Elohim Almighty and "that prophet" that God caused to speak whatever He said to him? If Jesus is 'That prophet' of Elohim, to not hear him would result in being "cut-off" from the brethren. If Paul taught a different message than Jesus or God – we should be running away from him – not founding thousands of competing churches upon his false testimony!]

The biggest lie in history:

[14] I am debtor both to the Greeks, and to the Barbarians; both to the wise, and to the unwise. [15] So, as much as in me is, I am ready to preach the gospel to you that are at Rome also. [16] For I am not ashamed of the gospel of Christ: for it is the power of God unto salvation to everyone that believeth; to the Jew first, and also to the Greek. [17] For therein is the righteousness of God revealed from faith to faith: as it is written, The just shall live by faith.

This is the general theme in Pauline theology, and I use the term "theology" because that is what he taught, his theory of the economy between salvation and damnation being about our "faith", as opposed to whether we are observing the will of God to do it – or not. If you read the words of God Himself, nowhere can we take the whole of His message and arrive at any such conclusion that "faith", as imagined and taught by Paul, is in any way equal to belonging to those Elohim said He will consider to be "My people." God revealed Himself and His will at Mount Sinai, everyone present agreed to His Standards – not from being compelled to by force, but by their desire to live their lives by the completely reasonable and upright standards He gave. Nothing complicated, nothing unreasonable, nothing undoable – and it included provision for forgiveness because God knows life is a growing process. We don't beat children learning to walk when they stumble, we help them up and encourage them to learn to do better. God is no different, except there are some things that are so evil as to be impossible to equate to just tripping or stumbling – true evil needs to be justly dealt with, but generally, forgiveness is based upon just restitution, not punishment or imprisonment. What "power" does God use to bring us to upright living but goodness, justice, reason, and true love that does no evil? That is no mystery – it's perfectly reasonable and is based on observation – not "faith" or "belief." The quote Paul uses here is generally agreed upon to be from Habacuc 2:4. The early church fathers' writings discovered in the Dead Sea Scrolls included this verse specifically because of Paul's claims – telling that the verse addresses "faithfulness," not "faith" alone as a separate entity. Another passage

misused by Paul is that Abraham believed God and it was accounted to him for righteousness – apart from the Law. Who accounted for who was righteous in the passage? If we read a bit further in Genesis 23 we can see that God was more specific to tell Abraham's heir that it was because of Abraham's obedience, his faithfulness, not his "belief", or "faith." Recall, the first principles Jesus taught were about uprightly handling the words of God – to live by every word that proceeds from the mouth of God, to not tempt God to keep His word and not pit one word of God against another – which means to understand His words are in harmony when properly understood and applied (observed). Paul's assumptions herein prove he had no understanding of the first lessons of Jesus in the Temptation account.

What is your "faith", but what you believe? That there are thousands of churches proves they don't have the same "faith" or "belief", even though all claim to believe in Jesus. If Jesus is true, it is about being faithful disciples who learn from him and abide in his words and the words of the Father and that we serve the Father, not Jesus – we rather are yoked with Jesus to serve God when we are his disciples indeed.

God's Wrath Against Sinful Humanity

[18] For the wrath of God is revealed from heaven against all ungodliness and unrighteousness of men, who hold the truth in unrighteousness;[19] Because that which may be known of God is manifest in them; for God hath shewed it unto them.[20] For the invisible things of him from the creation of the world are clearly seen, being understood by the things that are made, even his eternal power and Godhead; so that they are without excuse:

We must recall that in the days of Paul, there was no "Bible" in the home of every believer, let alone mankind, throughout the ancient world. Scriptures were rare and only available to a select few. There are still many on earth today who have no access to a Bible, or the education to read it. Public education since the 1800s has blessed most of the earth to now be able to read, and the printing press and the internet have opened up more avenues of knowledge and education than have ever existed in the known history of mankind. What Paul is doing here is building his straw-man. "Godless"? Having worked with thousands of people of every sort of belief and non-belief in California – I can attest that those from my own Church were often the ones who were the greatest problems, and their "belief" or "faith" in the gospel of Paul had much less influence on their morality than those without belief in God. One friend had a mother who instilled in him one simple rule to live by; she always asked him: "Are you sure you are doing the right thing?" They had a sense that it's wrong to lie, cheat, steal, defame, injure, or mess with the wife of another man – they had a God-given conscience that was not seared by the lies of Christianity – as many Christians use the cop-out from Paul that Jesus paid for their sins, and they, therefore, have been freed from the Law of God. So how did the untaught person know to live more uprightly than the religious persons? I submit it is because God was right when telling the Law/Covenant was no mystery, that it is indeed close to our hearts and our mouths – perhaps a direct proof that we were created in the image of God – as no other animal on the planet developed much of a conscience by nature. That the earth shows the handiwork of God is true, but human nature also shows the handiwork of God. The justice and mercy of God are also perfectly reasonable – so the truth is Paul invented a theology about God that does not reflect the truth of God that can be known by nature or Scripture. We need to be paying attention to the observable qualities of God and our fellow – not what is "invisible." Observe this: has evil ceased because Jesus died on the cross and resurrected – defeating Satan and sin? It is Paul who is without excuse, not mankind in general. As you read this next verse, recall the conversation God was having through Isaiah 1 of 'Come, let us reason together.' Some of the greatest evils ever done to mankind were done in the name of God by those who claimed the name, but failed to know Him or live as He had told them to.

[21] Because that, when they knew God, they glorified him not as God, neither were thankful; but became vain in their imaginations, and their foolish heart was darkened. [22] Professing themselves to be wise, they became fools, [23] And changed the glory of the incorruptible God into an image made like to corruptible man, and to birds, and four-footed beasts, and creeping things.

The evils done by Rome and Judaism are as bad as any on earth – pretending to serve the God of Abraham and Moses, or to believe in Jesus – all the while growing in their evil influence throughout mankind over their history. Mere belief or faith in God means nothing, shows nothing, is nothing – unless you make His Standards for life to be yours. I hope you are starting to realize Paul was inventing myth and lore – not "God-breathed Scripture" that was inspired or given via the Holy Spirit – is saying Paul taught the truth of God blasphemy against God? You'd better think carefully about who you believe. Also, notice some who believe in Paul's teachings have statues (idols?) that people often pray to – perhaps not believing Elohim capable of knowing their needs before they pray, or that He is so busy and limited that He requires dead saints to make petitions for the living? That is not the God that Jesus taught about. Isn't the truth that Elohim forbids communication with the dead? Jesus taught us how to pray.

[24] Wherefore God also gave them up to uncleanness through the lusts of their own hearts, to dishonor their own bodies between themselves:[25] Who changed the truth of God into a lie and worshipped and served the creature more than the Creator, who is blessed forever. Amen.[26] For this cause God gave them up unto vile affections: for even their women did change the natural use into that which is against nature:[27] And likewise, also the men, leaving the natural use of the woman, burned in their lust one toward another; men with men working that which is unseemly, and receiving in themselves that recompence of their error which was meet.

If Paul is true, doesn't that mean everyone who does not believe in his God is a homosexual and/or given over to abject unnatural depravity? If you believe Paul, you have to of necessity put blinders on your eyes so as to not see reality. It's crazy beliefs like this that cause many to look at Christians as deluded fanatics they want nothing to do with. Evangelical Christianity is one of the greatest lies ever told mankind in the name of God. Sin has consequences – good and evil have observable cause and effect. It also appears that the consequences extend beyond this life, as in the Covenant we find: "Blessed are you in your coming, and blessed are you in your going", and "Cursed are you in your coming, and cursed are you in your going." From where, and to where? The Psalms have some beautiful passages regarding this, and Psalm 1 introduces the entire book. "Praiseworthy is the man who walked not in the counsel of the wicked, and stood not in the path of the sinful, and sat not in the session of scorners. But his desire is in the Teachings of Elohim, and in His Law, he meditates day and night. He shall be like a tree deeply rooted alongside brooks of water, that yields its fruit in its season, and whose leaf never withers; and everything that he does will succeed. Not so wicked; rather they are like the chaff that the wind drives away. Therefore, the wicked shall not be vindicated in judgment, nor the sinful in the assembly of the righteous – for Elohim attends the way of the righteous, while the way of the wicked will perish." Evangelicals who judge others as evil because they don't believe the gospel of cheap grace will be in for a huge surprise when they hear: "Depart from me, you workers of lawlessness, I never knew you." We can look around today and see that those most blind to the evils happening in Israel are basically Evangelicals who support Israel's actions of many evils towards their fellow countrymen – the Palestinians. It's like they have blinders on and are paying no attention to the fact that all the Zionists hopes are based on prophecies that were fulfilled long ago – so much for what Gospel you believe proving if you are "saved" or not, let alone a better person by what you approve of and support!

[28] And even as they did not like to retain God in their knowledge, God gave them over to a reprobate mind, to do those things which are not convenient;[29] Being filled with all

unrighteousness, fornication, wickedness, covetousness, maliciousness; full of envy, murder, debate, deceit, malignity; whisperers,[30] Backbiters, haters of God, despiteful, proud, boasters, inventors of evil things, disobedient to parents,[31] Without understanding, covenant breakers, without natural affection, implacable, unmerciful:[32] Who knowing the judgment of God, that they which commit such things are worthy of death, not only do the same, but have pleasure in them that do them.

Jesus taught to repent to do the will of God. A very clear message, a message for those who need it – not assigning condemnation like a cement blanket. Paul was an idiot. As I've said before: God has spoken, and we need to hear Him. Jesus taught likewise. No one who works evil – the curses – knows or serves Elohim or knows the son. The evils of some religions, as Rome, and Judaism, show thousands of years of defying His Eternal Law. The focus of which is how we live towards our fellow shows our true relationship with Elohim.

Footnotes

a. Romans 1:3 Or *who according to the flesh*
b. Romans 1:4 Or *was declared with power to be the Son of God*
c. Romans 1:5 Or *that is*
d. Romans 1:13 The Greek word for *brothers and sisters (adelphoi)* refers here to believers, both men and women, as part of God's family; also in 7:1, 4; 8:12, 29; 10:1; 11:25; 12:1; 15:14, 30; 16:14, 17.
e. Romans 1:17 Or *is from faith to faith*
f. Romans 1:17 Hab. 2:4

One Disciple to Another review comments:

1:1-7. Note that no supporting passages are cited to support the gospel as taught by Paul. Subtext comments lack support to any of the gospel accounts in the New Testament – let alone the need to find alignment to the teachings of Jesus in Matthew – both are nonexistent. The supporting passages are to writings attributed to Paul, and per the Instruction of Jesus and God, the teachings would have to find accord with theirs. Since no verifying witness is provided, the Standard God gave is violated, as even Jesus said if he testified to himself, without supporting testimony – his testimony would not be true. So how can we accept the testimony of Paul without like supporting witness as is found in Jesus' teachings? It is needful to keep the gospel of Matthew in mind, as the Hebrew gospel of Matthew was accepted by the Jerusalem Church before 40 CE while the apostles were still around. Since the HGOM predates Paul's letters, it could have provided

needful information to Paul of what Yeshua (Jesus) taught his disciples. Was Paul teaching as Jesus taught when he claims the gospel of salvation by grace through faith? We must note who Paul claimed to teach obedience to, and then double check what God and Jesus had to say to us and see if Paul remained true to the "tests" God commanded we use. This is vital to keep in mind as we review Romans. Jesus taught that faith results in obedience and is one of the weightier matters of the Law, and obedience is to be doing the will of God, as stated in the Everlasting Covenant, and supporting Scripture in the Torah, Prophets and Psalms. Jesus taught nothing new, and his teachings can be found in accord with the instructions of God and the rest of the Holy Scripture of his day (Dead Sea Scrolls, proto-Deuteronomy, and Hebrew Scripture). Can the teachings of Paul also be shown to be true to God as the Teachings of Jesus in Matthew?

A side thought is what Paul claims of the Spirit. Was Jesus' birth said to have been accomplished by the Spirit, as Mary had known no man? (HGOM and GGOM). Which gospel claims Yeshua was resurrected by the Holy Spirit? "through the Spirit of holiness was appointed the Son of God in power[b] by his resurrection from the dead." God showed Jesus as approved and to be representing Him by the miracles he performed and in His statements at his baptism and the transfiguration – they are witnessing that God gave to him – as God also did to Moses and other prophets.

What did God say at Sinai about those who love Him and keep His commandments? His words from Sinai are clear to define who He says who is blessed, as well as who He said are cursed. This is my accounting of the consolidated Covenant Standards of the Ten Decrees, Blessed, and Cursed, reportedly 3000 years old and published in 2021. Let's keep the words of God in mind as we review the claims of Saul/Paul, and for the teachings of Jesus.

I am Elohim, your god, who freed you from the land of Egypt, from the slave-house. You shall not have any other gods. You shall not make a carving or any image that is in the heavens above or the earth below or in the waters beneath the earth. You shall not prostrate yourselves before them, and you shall not serve them. Blessed is the man who has Elohim as his god, and who prostrates himself only to him, and who serves him alone. Cursed is the man who does a carving or a casting, the handiwork of a craftsman. I am Elohim, your god.

Sanctify the seventh day and rest on it. For in six days, I made the heavens and the earth and all that is in them, and I rested on the seventh day. Therefore, you too shall rest, along with your livestock and all that you have. Blessed is the man who sanctifies the seventh day and rests on it. Cursed is the man who does work on the seventh day I am Elohim, your god.

Honor your father and your mother. Blessed is he who honors his father and his mother. Cursed is he who disgraces his father and mother. I am Elohim, your god.

You shall not slay the soul of your brother. Blessed is the man who does not avenge or exact retribution for the soul of his brother. Cursed is he who strikes down his fellow in secret. I am Elohim, your god.

You shall not commit adultery with the wife of your fellow. Blessed is the man who does not defile the wife of his fellow. Cursed is the man who approaches any of his kin, or who commits adultery with the wife (woman) of his fellow, or who copulates with any animal. I am Elohim, your god.

You shall not steal the property of your brother. Blessed is the man who does not cheat his fellow. Cursed is he who moves the boundary marker of his fellow. I am Elohim, your God.

You shall not swear in my name falsely, for I shall avenge the transgression of the fathers against the sons, grandsons, and great grandsons for those who bear my name falsely. Blessed is the man who does not swear in my name falsely. Cursed is the man who swears falsely in my name. I am Elohim, your god.

You shall not submit against your fellow a false judgment. Blessed is the man who does not deceive or lie to his fellow. Cursed is he who takes a bribe to give false judgment against his comrade. I am Elohim, your god.

You shall not desire the woman of your fellow, his male servant, his female servant, or anything that is his. Blessed is he who does not lust after anyone belonging to his fellow. Cursed is the man who desires and lusts after the woman of his fellow, his daughter, his female servant, or anything that is his. I am Elohim, your god.

You shall not hate your brother in your heart. Blessed is the man who loves his fellow. Cursed is the man who hates his brother in his heart. I am Elohim, your god.

It is these ten pronouncements that Elohim uttered to you upon the mountain from amid the fire. Blessed is the man who upholds all the proclamations of this teaching to perform them. Cursed is the man who does not uphold all the proclamations of this teaching to perform them.

Had Israel been infused with the knowledge of the Covenant, there is no way that the Ten Decrees could have been altered by the corrupted priesthood and scribes near the time of Ezekiel, and the obvious fact "V" tells is that they did, and all should repent to believe the unaltered words given by Elohim, which are now restored after almost 3000 years!!!! Jesus did teach according to the Original Decrees - as we can note his sayings about what one calls another - such as "you fool!" to be a dangerous thing to do - which is in total accord with "You shall not hate your brother in your heart. I am Elohim, your god." (the deleted commandment)

We must also note who God declared "Blessed" or "Cursed", as we consider these things every day, in what we say and do. As for me, I choose to believe God is true to His word - but not the alterations of the Pharisees or Rome. Our hope should be that, as God told Cain, he was responsible and capable to repent and do rightly to be in proper relationship with both God and his brother. May Elohim be merciful towards those who did the best they could with what they were able to know, but surely, since we can now know - we must surely repent to believe His words as given, not as altered by those of the evil one - who was cursed for doing so! As Isaiah 42 foretells: Restore!

"Blessed are you in the field, blessed are you in the city, blessed are your firstling and your remnant. Blessed are the fruit of your loins and the fruit of your land, the wombs of your cattle and the bellies of your sheep. Blessed are you in your coming, and blessed are you in your going. Elohim will set your enemies - defeated - before you. Elohim will order blessing upon all your handiwork. Elohim will establish you as a holy people, all the peoples of the land will behold and fear you. Elohim will open the heavens for you, to give rain for your land in its season. You will lend to many nations: you will not borrow. You will be only on top: you will not be on the bottom. Elohim will make you abound only in goodness upon the good land that Elohim, God of your fathers, is giving you."

"The Levites shall continue calling out in a loud voice and say, If you do not heed the voice of Elohim, taking care to do all his commandments and decrees, then all of these curses will befall you:

Cursed are you in the city, cursed are you in the field, cursed are your firstling and your remnant. Cursed are the fruit of your loins and the fruit of your land, the wombs of your cattle and the bellies of your sheep. Cursed are you in your coming, and cursed are you in your going. Elohim will set you - defeated - before your enemies. Elohim will cast the execration upon all your handiwork. Elohim will make you an epitaph, a proverb, and a saying among all the nations of the land. Elohim will stop up the heavens.

The stranger settled in your midst will rise higher and higher; your will descend lower and lower. He will lend it to you; you will not lend to him. Elohim will demolish and eradicate you from the land that you are going into to possess.

...... **Be strong and resolute; do not fear and do not panic. For Elohim, your god - he is the one who walks alongside you. He will not let go of you; he will not abandon you. Now write down this teaching, so that <u>this teaching may be a witness before you, since it will not be forgotten from the mouths of your descendants, for I know the schemes that you devise.</u>**

These are the words that Moses instructed all the children of Israel according to the order of YHWH on the plains of Moab before his death.

Romans 2
God's Righteous Judgment

1. Therefore, thou art inexcusable, O man, whosoever thou art that judges: for wherein thou judges another, thou condemns thyself; for thou that judges does the same things.

[The Law is the set Standard for living justly. It's a common ploy of a guilty person to accuse another of what they do – as we've all seen in the Democratic Party and Deep State accusing Trump of collusion with the Russians when, in fact, they are the ones who were colluding against Trump and the people of the United States of America. Another notable example is Judaism's bigoted history that resulted in the formation of the ADL, told in 3 volumes of "The Secret Relationship Between Blacks and Jews." Read your Bible. Revisit the words of God in Isaiah 1 and Ezekiel 18. Note that many have never testified falsely, stolen from another, committed adultery, or idol worshippers. Records in our scriptures indicate God viewed idol worship to be worship of demons – not mere pieces of wood, stone, clay, or metal. Few are likely to have gone around coveting the property of others – why covet when you can earn your own money and buy what you want? Paul is making blanket false accusations – which is what Satan does – as "Satan" means accuser – and from what I've observed so far – a false accuser. Paul gave no proof to show his charges against everyone were true. Even if one were to violate a commandment of God, God commanded forgiveness when the conditions for forgiveness were fulfilled! Repeatedly He said: "And so he shall be forgiven." It was those who refused to forgive when God said to forgive that were "cut off", not the penitent sinner. Paul is exhibiting total disregard for the Law, not knowing the first principles of distinguishing between good and evil. For the Law to be just, it must be about judgment – discernment of good and evil. Saying everyone is guilty and therefore cannot judge others without condemning ourselves. We all do not do the same things – those of Elohim choose to do what He said is good and blessed – and Jesus taught the same thing. This is also the value of the teaching about communication if we think we have offended someone, or if we believe they have offended us – that we speak about it and seek to make things right – the way God and Jesus said to. Paul's viewpoint here is against the Law – "Lawlessness".]

[2] But we are sure that the judgment of God is according to truth against them which commit such things.[3] And thickest thou this, O man, that judges them which do such things, and does the same, that thou shalt escape the judgment of God?[4] Or despises thou

the riches of his goodness and forbearance and longsuffering; not knowing that the goodness of God leadeth thee to repentance?

[God does not forgive without true repentance – read the Torah – see what God said! See what Jesus said. Forgiveness follows repentance – not the other way around!!! Paul has reversed the ways of God!! It is true that His kindness, or graciousness, should lead us to repentance, but denial of His Instruction regarding the Covenant Standards will have no good end, and it is wrong to judge short of, or beyond, what He decreed. It's a no brainer to say God is just, but what is the intent Paul in posing here?]

Paul is making many false presumptions against the words of God and the teachings of Jesus. To understand the gospel message, it is necessary to first read and comprehend the Hebrew Gospel of Matthew to know what he taught. This is the link to the Hebrew Gospel of Matthew and supporting texts from the pre-existing Hebrew Scripture of his day. http://www.onediscipletoanother.org/id6.html

The core Teachings of Yeshua are in the Sermon on the Mount, so at least review chapters 5-7 to know them, as Paul is defying them already. Yeshua's teaching was in accord with the words of God. We are to judge according to the judgment God gave us from Sinai and through Moses – and accept that Jesus was restoring them and giving their proper interpretation and application for the lives of his disciples. If we judge in accord to the words of God – it is doing the will of God – it is accepting His judgments, as we also accept what He declared just restitution to be performed by those who "keep His word", and as He decreed: "And so he shall be forgiven" – repeatedly commanded by God in Leviticus. If we do not judge according to His decree and justice, we are spurning or ignoring His justice and mode of maintaining an orderly, just and merciful society among those who claim His NAME – those He said are "My people." Judgment is part of the commandments of God so we can be found by Him to have been living justly, to have loved mercy, and to have been walking humbly with our God through the obvious TRUTH that He decreed we use for our manner of life to possess His kindness and to also reside in His love and care. All the ways of God are pure, just and true – He gave us wonderful standards to live by. Read Psalm 119 and see what David had to say about the Law of God. No wonder God said David was a man who was approved by Him, and man after His own heart – showing God does weigh the hearts of men, that He desires all to repent of evil, and that His graciousness is shown in His Instructions to help us be better people – indeed, that we become all He intended for us from the beginning!!!

Psalm 1, Hebrew to English, Stone Edition:

"Praiseworthy is the man who walked not in the counsel of the wicked, and stood not in the path of the sinful, and sat not in the session of scorners. But his desire is in the Torah (Teachings) of Elohim, and in His Torah (Teachings) he meditates day and night. He shall be like a tree deeply rooted alongside brooks of water, that yields its fruit in its season, and whose leaf never withers; and everything that he does will succeed. Not so wicked, rather they are like the chaff that the wind drives away. Therefore, the wicked shall not be vindicated in judgment, nor the sinful in the assembly of the righteous – for Elohim attends the way of the righteous, while the way of the wicked will perish."]

[5]But after thy hardness and impenitent heart treasures up unto thyself wrath against the day of wrath and revelation of the righteous judgment of God.

[God revealed Himself and His Instruction in Righteousness at Sinai and supporting Scripture! There is no waiting to know what God has already revealed! It appears to be Paul and his disciples who will be in for a stark awakening to the Truth of God and His faithfulness to His word and covenant. If the Bereans had Romans and Galatians in their hands, they should have been able to see that what Paul said is NOT according to the word of God or Jesus' teachings from God. Dare we judge Paul according to the word of God – and according to the teachings of Jesus in Matthew?]

[6]Who will render to every man according to his deeds: [7]To them who by patient continuance in well doing seek for glory and honor and immortality, eternal life: [8]But unto them that are contentious, and do not obey the truth, but obey unrighteousness, indignation and wrath, [9]Tribulation and anguish, upon every soul of man that doeth evil, of the Jew first, and also of the Gentile; [10]But glory, honor, and peace, to every man that worketh good, to the Jew first, and also to the Gentile: [11] For there is no respect of persons with God.

[God deserves all the glory and honor – according to God and the Teachings of Yeshua (Jesus). Those who place their judgments above what God decreed – by either ignoring, adding to, or subtracting from His stated standards given to live by are those who are not being faithful to God, or proper consideration of their fellow mankind. This is why Jesus' first Teaching is that "Man shall not live by bread alone, but by every word that proceeds from the mouth of God." As for "First to the Jew, then to the Gentile", both were present at Sinai, both ratified the Everlasting Covenant at the same time, and the same Law was for all men and includes distinction for some things between the offspring of Abraham, Isaac and Jacob, but in matters of living justly and loving mercy – the Covenant has certain conditions and was never unconditional. It is because God does not show favoritism that both were present at Sinai. It is because of the promise of God to Abraham's descendants that possession of the land was for the faithful children of Israel. As for the instruction of God, He said, regarding keeping the Law: "Choose life, that ye might live!" When God gave the Covenant at Sinai, it was to bless men of all nations!!!]

¹² For as many as have sinned without law shall also perish without law: and as many as have sinned in the law shall be judged by the law; ¹³ (For not the hearers of the law are just before God, but the doers of the law shall be justified. ¹⁴ For when the Gentiles, which have not the law, do by nature the things contained in the law, these, having not the law, are a law unto themselves: ¹⁵ Which shew the work of the law written in their hearts, their conscience also bearing witness, and their thoughts the mean while accusing or else excusing one another;) ¹⁶ In the day when God shall judge the secrets of men by Jesus Christ <u>according to my gospel.</u>

In these verses Paul brushes up against a truth that is universal and then takes his train off the tracks – very odd indeed. Regarding the Law, God declared it very near to us, in our hearts and mouths. The most obvious thing would be to consider the last eight of the Ten Declarations being in our nature to keep, as we know when we have been wronged, and should therefore not do to others what we would consider to have been a wrong against us: false testimony against us, murder of a loved one, stealing that which belongs to us, defiling the marriage bed, or others being jealous of our possessions and looking for ways to take them from us or to treat us badly because they don't have what we have – which could well lead to a number of wrongs. In this limited sense the Law God declared is very near us if we have not been so abused as to deny what is built into our basic nature by our Maker. One Law is for all, and most people will have heard the shortened version of the Ten Commandments and never pondered the full account as given by God that included the Blessings and the Curses. In a normal state of humanity people can live upright lives and not commit evil, but do they realize that God, who created man, is the one that they can thank for creating us in His image – above all the other creations of the earth to possess an innate sense of right and wrong and morality and capable to define some system of justice?

These matters are unique to humans of all the creatures on earth, and man is at his lowest when he denies his higher self to then behave as a mere animal, and sometimes worse! These things are to take place during our lives if we open our eyes to observe reality. If these things take place in our lives – and the lives of others for thousands of years – how is it that Paul says: "¹⁶ This will take place on the day when God judges people's secrets through Jesus Christ, as my gospel declares."? The Torah is no "secret". Matthew is no "secret." God was open and

transparent to give us just and reasonable standards to live and judge by – that we do the truth by relying on His revealed Standards/Law for our manner of life and justice.

The Jews and the Law

[17] Behold, thou art called a Jew, and restest in the law, and makest thy boast of God, [18] And knowest his will, and approves the things that are more excellent, being instructed out of the law; [19] And art confident that thou thyself art a guide of the blind, a light of them which are in darkness, [20] An instructor of the foolish, a teacher of babes, which hast the form of knowledge and of the truth in the law. [21] Thou therefore which teaches another, teaches thou not thyself? thou that preaches a man should not steal, dost thou steal? [22] Thou that sayest a man should not commit adultery, dost thou commit adultery? thou that abhorrest idols, dost thou commit sacrilege? [23] Thou that makest thy boast of the law, through breaking the law dishonors thou God? [24] For the name of God is blasphemed among the Gentiles through you, as it is written.

I'm continually surprised of the respect for Paul that was drilled and mentally beaten into me as a child – perhaps this is why I have so little regard towards his writings and write these reviews today – to free others of trusting in his nonsense and lies against God and those that God says should be considered to be "My people." I don't think Paul/Saul capable to handle any God given principle uprightly in any of his writings, but perhaps one will be found. Do all teachers of the Law commit such sins?! Evil characters exist in Christianity, Judaism and Islam – if evil is what God declared to be evil – if the word of God is true – no one should brand all as evil because all are not evil and all do not reject His word. As Ezekiel 18 clearly says, each person is responsible for their own sins. If God declared this through Ezekiel, who is accepted to have been a true prophet, we should exercise judgment to not condemn those that God said are "My people" – whether Jew or non-Jew. Israel is a nation before God. Other nations come and go – and God has no regard for nations – but does regard what each man does – whether he will obey God – or not. The references to this section include Isaiah and Ezekiel. Paul would have done well to support that thousands of people have lived just and righteous lives in the eyes of God and encourage all to repent to do the will of God with all their heart, mind, body, soul and strength. As for Jews – they don't believe Christians account of Jesus because Christians deny the Laws of God and have altered the Hebrew Scripture. If you don't believe the book of Mormon because it doesn't keep to the Christian Bible – you should easily see why Jews don't believe Christians when they have altered the words of God and pretend their account is true because the Pope declared it so and publishers published it as a "Bible". Both Isaiah and Ezekiel wrote their message to a fallen

and corrupted Israel. To judge all Jews today for the sins of their "fathers" is to violate Ezekiel 18 and the Law. Also, God has not been without grace towards man since the "fall", as told to Cain, Noah, giving His Covenant through Moses, and through Ezekiel, the evil man who turns to do righteousness will be forgiven as though the sins were not committed, just as the righteous man who turns from his righteousness to then do evil – his righteousness will not be remembered. In the Hebrew gospel of Matthew, Yeshua taught the same principles about forgiveness as had been revealed in the Hebrew Scriptures. The idea some Christians have of "eternal security" or "once saved, always saved" is in direct opposition to the decree and word of God. To the unsuspecting Paul seems to be someone to believe, but after a life of trying to live by his standards – I can certainly testify against every one of his writings to have twisted the word of God and to be nothing but the imaginations of a deluded man. As for the NAME of God being blasphemed by others because of Judaism's evils and bigotry, the matter initiates from the "Law." Elohim said it is about the conditions of the Sinai Covenant. Judaism says it is about the 1200 CE invented "613 Laws", instead of the 10. Judaism also says for non-Jews, they are to keep the "7 Noahide Laws" invented by the same Rabbi. Both of these account deny that it is about the 10 given in the Sinai Covenant and also told in Isaiah 56 to be the same Standards for those of any nationality – this defies Rabbinic Judaism, and shows it to have absolutely corrupted their minds from the simplicity and beauty of the Everlasting Covenant. I've looked up each of the 613 and found them to be supremely absent of the sense of goodness, common sense, and humanity in the words of God. The list with references is in the study helps of the Aramaic English New Testament, by Andrew Roth. Check them out for yourself – it was patently obvious to me, but you are certainly entitled and encouraged to see if what I say here is true – or not.

[25] For circumcision verily profited, if thou keep the law: but if thou be a breaker of the law, thy circumcision is made uncircumcision.[26] Therefore if the uncircumcision keep the righteousness of the law, shall not his uncircumcision be counted for circumcision? [27] And shall not uncircumcision which is by nature, if it fulfills the law, judge thee, who by the letter and circumcision dost transgress the law?

As God declared when giving the Law, there is one Law for both the circumcised and the uncircumcised. The Law is the conditions for the Everlasting Covenant made and ratified at Sinai by the Children of Israel and the "multitude of nations" preserved by God from Egypt to Sinai. Yes, if we observe the Law – whether Jewish, or not – we reside in the kindness and blessings of God. If we break the Law – whether Jewish, or not – we bring judgment upon ourselves as noted in the Law. God made distinctions in the Law that show breaking particular matters have different consequences, depending on the severity of the matter broken – the penalties were not universal condemnation and eternal damnation for minor issues. The matter is that all who call upon His NAME as their God are to make the Law the universal manner of life Guide for us as He gave it – not altering it to either diminish or add to it. Circumcision was no aid to a Jew who broke the Law, but to be a Jew and not be circumcised was to break the Abrahamic Covenant – in fact, circumcision is a pre-law condition reportedly given to Abraham. Circumcision is not in the "Law", it was another Covenant and about the Land – if they were faithful to the Sinai "Law" Covenant. To be a Law keeper requires the system of justice as commanded by God, including the provisions for mercy – as given by God – such as Joseph not desiring to put away Mary. Note that God is specific to say what sin is, and in Paul we have nothing but imaginations such as what is "expedient" or that whatever one believes to be a sin is a sin – regardless of what God declared!! Although God never commanded perfection to attain to His glory to any man, this is what we hear from Paul in "for all have sinned and fallen short of the glory of God". Paul was truly a very tricky character and the likely source of most all divisions in Christianity have some root in a doctrine from Paul. Just look at the Doctrinal Statements for each Church or Sect of Christianity and how many supporting passages are from Paul – rather than the words of God and the Anointed One – "Son of man". Perhaps the best passage to observe exactly what God said about those of all nations who are not Hebrews is Isaiah 56 – it's explicit.

[28]For he is not a Jew, which is one outwardly; neither is that circumcision, which is outward in the flesh:

Keeping the Law was universal to all God said are "My people" – whether Jewish, or not – this is clearly the only conclusion that agrees with the words of God. If you don't believe it – prove it by the words of God in the Hebrew Scripture and the Dead Sea Scrolls Bible. The Christian published Bible is not reliable enough to trust in many key passages quoted in the New Testament, such as Isaiah 7:14. See "Let's Get Biblical" volumes 1 and 2. Watch some of Rabbi Tovia Singer's videos on YouTube. Singer makes many good points to prove the matter but do keep the Teachings of Jesus in Matthew front and center as you consider what Singer says. Recall the words of God in the Ten Decrees – Paul is testifying against God. God wrote the Ten Decrees on stone – not a material that decomposes and passes away with time. The Law is the standard those of God will observe to do. Being a Jew is about the bloodline descendants of Abraham, Isaac and Jacob. God preserved the "multitude of nations" from Egypt with Israel, and both were given and ratified the same Covenant at Sinai with Elohim. Those who serve God alone, keep His sabbath and who grasp His covenant tightly (Isaiah 56) are those He said will be blessed. His favor is not based on whether you are Jewish or not. Where did Jesus or God talk about "circumcision of the heart"? If they did – see what they had to say about it, then you will have no need to be misled by Paul.

²⁹But he is a Jew, which is one inwardly; and circumcision is that of the heart, in the spirit, and not in the letter; whose praise is not of men, but of God.

In this verse Paul says it is the "Spirit" who circumcises the heart. Ezekiel 37 says God gave His Spirit to write the Law upon the heart as an aid to keep it. Didn't God say He gives His Spirit to those who obey Him? Obey what? Obey the manner of life that God says His people will live – the Law/Covenant Standards. Obedience is to grow in our knowledge of the will of God and to continue in our faithfulness to make His will to be our will. This is our work: to believe God and repent to live just and reasonable lives that are in accord with His Everlasting Covenant – and as Jesus/Joshua 2 taught – to "live by every word that proceeds from the mouth of God; and in his prayer that "Thy will be done on earth as it is in Heaven." To be a "Jew" is to be of the seed of the flesh of Abraham. Get a genetic test kit to see if you are a Jew or not – it's that simple for us today. Then do as God taught and commanded. A note regarding the footnotes – see the DSSB and Hebrew Scriptures. The Septuagint (LXX) was not accepted by Jews because it was poorly done – reality is not what we have been taught. Our scholars have failed us. The Jewish translation to Greek of the Hebrew Scripture was only the Torah and did not include Isaiah or Ezekiel, and it was burned in a fire long ago. The Hebrew Gospel of Matthew, which preceded the Greek translation and alteration, used the Hebrew Scriptures, not the LXX. Due to the texts that are mistranslated in the LXX (Greek), there is no doubt in my mind that the LXX is a work of disciples of Paul – not Jews who knew the Hebrew language. Life is a process, and as Elohim told Cain: "Surely, if you improve yourself, you will be forgiven." He said we are capable to overcome our faults if sin has not overtaken us – that we are both capable and responsible to "improve ourselves." Rather than figuring all you had to do was "Claim the Name of Jesus" – you need to awaken from Pauline slumber/bewitchment to realize you need to look at your own life honestly and determine where you need to abandon evil and learn to do good. Examine the Standards of the Decrees and see they are all fair, upright, reasonable and are doable by anyone of good will.

Footnotes

a. Romans 2:6 Psalm 62:12; Prov. 24:12
b. Romans 2:24 Isaiah 52:5 (see Septuagint); Ezek. 36:20,22
c. Romans 2:27 *Or who, by means of a*

Romans 3
God's Faithfulness

³ What advantage then hath the Jew? or what profit is there of circumcision?² Much every way: chiefly, because that unto them were committed the oracles of God.³ For what if some did not believe? shall their unbelief make the faith of God without effect?⁴ God forbid: yea, let God be true, but every man a liar; as it is written, That thou mightiest be justified in thy sayings, and mightiest overcome when thou art judged.⁵ But if our unrighteousness commend the righteousness of God, what shall we say? Is God unrighteous who taketh vengeance? (I speak as a man)⁶ God forbid: for then how shall God judge the world?⁷ For if the truth of God hath more abounded through my lie unto his glory; why yet am I also judged as a sinner?⁸ And not rather, (as we be slanderously reported, and as some affirm that we say,) Let us do evil, that good may come? whose damnation is just.

No One Is Righteous

⁹What then? are we better than they? No, in no wise: for we have before proved both Jews and Gentiles, that they are all under sin; ¹⁰As it is written, There is none righteous, no, not one: ¹¹There is none that understandeth, there is none that seeketh after God.¹²They are all gone out of the way, they are together become unprofitable; there is none that doeth good, no, not one. ¹³Their throat is an open sepulchre; with their tongues they have used deceit; the poison of asps is under their lips: ¹⁴Whose mouth is full of cursing and bitterness: ¹⁵Their feet are swift to shed blood: ¹⁶Destruction and misery are in their ways: ¹⁷And the way of peace have they not known: ¹⁸There is no fear of God before their eyes. ¹⁹Now we know that what things soever the law saith, it saith to them who are under the law: that every mouth may be stopped, and all the world may become guilty before God. ²⁰Therefore by the deeds of the law there shall no flesh be justified in his sight: for by the law is the knowledge of sin.

Well, I've never been able to note anywhere God said any such thing. The Teachings of Jesus were noted in "One Disciple to Another" to have many references to the Hebrew Scripture that says the opposite, that keeping the conditions to the Everlasting Covenant is our righteousness – whether Jew or Gentile. References to each of the Beatitudes prove this is true. We need to observe what God said sin is if we desire to honor God as true. We also need to note what God declared holy, and also what God declared to be evil, as He said to "do no evil." One should easily see that the words of God are His "gracious instruction in righteousness." Ignorance is no excuse from the Law. Jesus said his disciples are

to keep the Law, and that unless our righteousness exceeds that of the scribes and Pharisees of his day that we cannot enter the kingdom of God by ANY means! Is Paul teaching something different? Has no one else read the Torah?! Paul's accounting of his gospel seems to be "fake News", not true religion that lives by the word of God. How is one to reconcile this passage of Paul to Ezekiel 18, or other places where Paul is defying the words of God? I doubt one can find a Jewish Rabbi that would consider Paul anything but a biblical ignoramus or a bold two-faced liar. Should you find one who doesn't, you should greatly question his being honest with you.

Righteousness Through Faith

[21]But now the righteousness of God without the law is manifested, being witnessed by the law and the prophets; [22]Even the righteousness of God which is by faith of Jesus Christ unto all and upon all them that believe: for there is no difference: [23]For all have sinned, and come short of the glory of God; [24]Being justified freely by his grace through the redemption that is in Christ Jesus: [25]Whom God hath set forth to be a propitiation through faith in his blood, to declare his righteousness for the remission of sins that are past, through the forbearance of God; [26]To declare, I say, at this time his righteousness: that he might be just, and the justifier of him which believeth in Jesus. [27]Where is boasting then? It is excluded. By what law? of works? Nay: but by the law of faith. [28]Therefore we conclude that a man is justified by faith without the deeds of the law. [29]Is he the God of the Jews only? is he not also of the Gentiles? Yes, of the Gentiles also: [30]Seeing it is one God, which shall justify the circumcision by faith, and uncircumcision through faith.[31] Do we then make void the law through faith? God forbid: yea, we establish the law.

Where did God or Jesus ever say a baby is born a sinner? Where did God say any man must match 'the glory of God' to be seen as a righteous person? Jesus scolded the religious leaders of his day for majoring in minors (tithing) and neglecting weightier matters of the Law – which absolutely included faith and doing the will of God as He gave it to start with – not as modified or taught around by the Rabbi. Faith is of the Law. Jesus said when we do the will of God that our good deeds are to be observed by others so that they will glorify God – not for our boasting! God, Jesus, and all the Law, Prophets and Psalms affirm that if one loves God, one must observe His instruction in righteousness and do no evil. God said those who are His enemies are those who reject His law – rejected knowledge. Paul is lying here – if God is true. Paul is doing nothing but the work of Satan – trying to cause you to think God said other than He clearly said, as well as testifying against the Gospel as taught by Jesus! You are not an illiterate soul if you are reading this. Don't take my word for it – read your Bible – do some study – as we've been lied to by "Christian" scholars and publishers

about this. If you want to pay to hear the message to reject the goodness of the blessed words of God and Jesus – by all means – ignore the words of God! However – ignorance is no excuse, as the time for ignorance has long passed. Looks like the time of the Gentiles is up, as they reject the instruction of God and that Prophet – to believe the nonsense of Paul and Rome. Am I to be considered a liar because I'm telling the truth on God and Jesus? Will you also hate the truth taught by Jesus? Do you want to remain in the dark prison houses manufactured to keep you deluded from the Truth?

In which Gospel did Jesus declare himself to be the blood sacrifice for the sins of mankind? In which prophecy did God declare He would make His only Son to be a blood sacrifice for the sins of mankind? How can this be true if God said those of Israel who offered the fruit of their body for the sins of their souls to have been evil – and done that which had never entered the mind of God? God said so – so if it had NEVER entered His mind – then how is Jesus "the lamb slain from the foundation of the world"? In which prophecy does God declare "that prophet" or "the son of man" or "the son of David" to be a sin offering for the world to excuse all who believe such nonsense?! Do tell –search it out to the Hebrew Scripture, Dead Sea Scrolls and the original Zodiac, Enoch, Job and Jubilees! Paul is a liar, and if he knew Hebrew, he lied about it – as "seed" is always plural – not singular as taught in his nonsense gospel of pretended grace and 'seed' versus 'seeds'. No wonder Jesus declared he will tell many "depart from me, ye who reject the Torah", as "anomia" *iniquity is to be against or without the Torah (Law).

Footnotes

a. Romans 3:4 Psalm 51:4
b. Romans 3:12 Psalms 14:1-3; 53:1-3; Eccles. 7:20
c. Romans 3:13 Psalm 5:9
d. Romans 3:13 Psalm 140:3
e. Romans 3:14 Psalm 10:7 (see Septuagint)
f. Romans 3:17 Isaiah 59:7,8
g. Romans 3:18 Psalm 36:1
h. Romans 3:22 Or *through the faithfulness of*
i. Romans 3:25 The Greek for sacrifice of atonement refers to the atonement cover on the ark of the covenant (see Lev. 16:15,16).

By all means – read all these support passages – in their entirety – and stop "cut and paste" religion that pits one verse against what God declared. Read Psalm 1, 2 and 119. Read Isaiah, Jeremiah, Ezekiel – read them all and see if you can find any support for what Paul taught! As Yeshua taught: blind leaders and blind followers will all fall in the same ditch. The main lesson from the Temptations account is to live by the words of God, don't tempt God to keep His word, and don't pit any teaching of God to be against another one – that within this framework you will be able to understand the proper interpretation and application of the Teachings God gave – and it may also be used to expose what teachings could not be from God.

Romans 4 NIV

[1]What then shall we say that Abraham, our forefather according to the flesh, discovered in this matter? [2]If, in fact, Abraham was justified by works, he had something to boast about—but not before God. [3]What does Scripture say? "Abraham believed God, and it was credited to him as righteousness."

What does Scripture say is the reason God found Abraham faithful to Him, that the promise continued through his son Isaac? Genesis 26: 2-5 defies this claim of Paul. Read your Bible – in fact, get the Hebrew Scriptures, and double check them that you rid yourself of Christian perversions of the Holy Scripture that altered any word of God. Genesis 15 is about Abraham having an heir. Genesis 17 is about the promise to bless all the nations through his seed – which was fulfilled at Sinai.

"Jehovah appeared to him and said, "Do not descend to Egypt; dwell in the land that I shall indicate to you. Sojourn in this land and I will be with you and bless you; for to you and your offspring will I give all these lands, and establish the oath that I swore to Abraham your father: 'I will increase your offspring like the stars of the heavens; and will give to your offspring all these lands'; and all the nations of the earth shall bless themselves by your offspring. Because Abraham obeyed My voice, and observed My safeguards, My commandments, My decrees, and My Torahs." (Prophecies were fulfilled long ago: Joshua 11:23; 12:7,8; 2 Samuel 8; 18; Joshua 26; 21:19,29; 27: 43-45; 23: 5,15; 24; Jeremiah 29:10; Ezra 1:1-5; Haggi 1,2; Ezra 6:3-5; Zacheriah 3:9; Jeremiah 2, 30. These are from some notes taken in haste – double check sources that are critical of Dispensational Theology – it is perhaps the latest developed theology in some Christian circles and stems from the Scofield Study Bibles, funded by Zionist Jews from the late 1800's and is currently promoted in many Evangelical circles.)

[4]Now to the one who works, wages are not credited as a gift but as an obligation. [5]However, to the one who does not work but trusts God who justifies the ungodly, their faith is credited as righteousness. [6]David says the same thing when he speaks of the blessedness of the one to whom God credits righteousness apart from works:

[7]"Blessed are those whose transgressions are forgiven, whose sins are covered. [8]Blessed is the one whose sin the Lord will never count against them."[b]

[9]Is this blessedness only for the circumcised, or also for the uncircumcised? We have been saying that Abraham's faith was credited to him as righteousness. [10]Under what

circumstances was it credited? Was it after he was circumcised, or before? It was not after, but before! ¹¹And he received circumcision as a sign, a seal of the righteousness that he had by faith while he was still uncircumcised. So then, he is the father of all who believe but have not been circumcised, in order that righteousness might be credited to them. ¹²And he is then also the father of the circumcised who not only are circumcised but who also follow in the footsteps of the faith that our father Abraham had before he was circumcised.

¹³It was not through the law that Abraham and his offspring received the promise that he would be heir of the world, but through the righteousness that comes by faith. ¹⁴For if those who depend on the law are heirs, faith means nothing and the promise is worthless, ¹⁵because the law brings wrath. And where there is no law there is no transgression.

¹⁶Therefore, the promise comes by faith, so that it may be by grace and may be guaranteed to all Abraham's offspring—not only to those who are of the law but also to those who have the faith of Abraham. He is the father of us all. ¹⁷As it is written: "I have made you a father of many nations."[c] He is our father in the sight of God, in whom he believed—the God who gives life to the dead and calls into being things that were not.

¹⁸Against all hope, Abraham in hope believed and so became the father of many nations, just as it had been said to him, "So shall your offspring be."[d] ¹⁹Without weakening in his faith, he faced the fact that his body was as good as dead—since he was about a hundred years old—and that Sarah's womb was also dead. ²⁰Yet he did not waver through unbelief regarding the promise of God but was strengthened in his faith and gave glory to God, ²¹being fully persuaded that God had power to do what he had promised. ²²This is why "it was credited to him as righteousness." ²³The words "it was credited to him" were written not for him alone, ²⁴but also for us, to whom God will credit righteousness—for us who believe in him who raised Jesus our Lord from the dead. ²⁵He was delivered over to death for our sins and was raised to life for our justification.

Footnotes

a. Romans 4:3 Gen. 15:6; also in verse 22
b. Romans 4:8 Psalm 32:1,2
c. Romans 4:17 Gen. 17:5
d. Romans 4:18 Gen. 15:5

Read the whole Psalm in context – what Paul said about it cannot be gained from reading the statement in context of the whole Psalm. Abraham believed and obeyed God; Abraham was not justified before God by faith alone or grace alone – but by faithfully doing as God instructed him. David never said God justifies His enemies – in fact, nowhere did God say such a thing. Prove this wrong if you

can – but do so by uprightly handling every word of God as given in the Hebrew Scriptures. If Jesus taught salvation by mere belief and trust in his death on the cross – why did he teach the need to repent and do as God instructed – to keep His commandments faithfully? Paul did nothing but twist the word of God to make up his own gospel, which defies the gospel taught by Jesus. Carefully note how absent the words of Jesus are in the writings of Saul. The best accounts of the Teachings of Jesus are in the Hebrew Gospel of Matthew, which was written before 40 CE, reportedly by his chosen emissaries, the apostles – the original disciples who were direct witnesses to his teachings, miracles, death, resurrection and ascent to Heaven to sit on the throne on the right hand of the Power on High – the Ancient of Days spoken of in Daniel. *Most importantly – nowhere in the Holy Scripture does God justify the ungodly*

Romans 5
Peace and Hope

KJV ¹Therefore being justified by faith, we have peace with God through our Lord Jesus Christ: ²By whom also we have access by faith into this grace wherein we stand and rejoice in hope of the glory of God. ³And not only so, but we glory in tribulations also: knowing that tribulation worketh patience; ⁴And patience, experience; and experience, hope: ⁵And hope maketh not ashamed; because the love of God is shed abroad in our hearts by the Holy Ghost which is given unto us.

God said He gives His Spirit to those who do His will – to those who obey Him. Ezekiel 37 is clear to say God gave the Spirit to write His words on our hearts to help us do them – not to excuse us from His instruction. We can hope in lies, or we can hope in the goodness of God towards those who observe His word that they might do it and make His instruction to be their manner and guide in life – to trust in His kindness towards those who love Him and keep His commandments. See Exodus 20. God defined love in the first commandment, and what Saul says above defies His definition. Saul is selling nothing but what the old-time false prophets taught: Peace! Peace! yet God said there is no peace for the lawless wicked. The peace of God resides in being faithful to the Everlasting Covenant and the Doctrine of God as taught by Yeshua. Believe Yeshua, or believe Saul/Paul – but no man can serve two masters. I'll choose to believe those who testify according to the words of God. Note the words of God in Ezekiel 34 about the shepherds that foul the waters of His sheep. Surely this is exactly what Paul has done to all who trust in his nonsense instead of the just and reliable words of God. Know it is NOT as taught by Paul – believe the word of God in Ezekiel 18! One need only observe Evangelical Christians support for Israel in Gaza, as the rest of the world looks on the same thing and say it is bad as any war crime in history – including Adolf Hitler – and I cringe to think they believe the Holy Spirit had anything to do with this idea... peace and hope???? Even the Pope has spoken out against it.

⁶For when we were yet without strength, in due time Christ died for the ungodly. ⁷For scarcely for a righteous man will one die: yet peradventure for a good man some would even dare to die. ⁸But God commended his love toward us, in that, while we were yet sinners, Christ died for us.

Who said we are powerless, without strength – aside from Paul? Did God say we are powerless? Did any true prophet say those who seek God in spirit and truth

are powerless? For that matter – man was not powerless after the "fall" in Eden. Rather than being powerless, God clearly told Cain that he was capable and responsible to rule over sin that it not rules over him! God clearly told Cain that by improving himself that he would be forgiven – elevated. Read the account in the Hebrew Scripture and the Dead Sea Scrolls. God made provision to forgive without blood sacrifice. Read Ezekiel 18.

⁹Much more then, being now justified by his blood, we shall be saved from wrath through him. ¹⁰For if, when we were enemies, we were reconciled to God by the death of his Son, much more, being reconciled, we shall be saved by his life. ¹¹And not only so, but we also joy in God through our Lord Jesus Christ, by whom we have now received the atonement.

Balderdash – this is nonsense. If Jesus (Yeshua) is our "Lord", we do as he commanded and instructed – which is to keep the Law and Covenant of God faithfully till death – to grow in producing the fruit that God created us to give to Him – because man was created in the image of God! Although everything belongs to Him already, living as He instructed is certainly a blessing to ourselves and to all those we live with, but first that we receive of the kindness and blessing of God Almighty. The primary issues exposed in the Teachings of Jesus are these major alterations foisted upon us all for almost 2000 years:

1. **There is no vicarious or substitutionary atonement – the righteousness of the righteous is not imputed to the ungodly, wicked and sinners who rebel against the Ten Decrees of God. Neither will God hold the righteous accountable for the sins of the wicked or those who spurn His instruction.**

2. **Yeshua made no claim to be Divine, but clearly spoke of himself as mortal – which is what "son of man" means.**

3. **The godly life is a process of growing – not something attained by a mere prayer any more than eating a magic cracker or sipping from a magic cup.**

4. **God never declared man totally depraved because of the "fall" of Adam and Eve – this is a total invention. Shouldn't we instead believe the words God spoke to Cain also apply to us? Seems very reasonable to me.**

Death Through Adam, Life Through Christ

¹²Wherefore, as by one man sin entered into the world, and death by sin; and so death passed upon all men, for that all have sinned:

God doesn't apply the sins of one person to another (vicarious atonement) – see Ezekiel 18, look through the prophets and Psalms and observe this was not said by others, and when the prophets spoke of everyone sinning it was because in their day that is what was going on – it was not a universal condemnation.

¹³(For until the law sin was in the world: but sin is not imputed when there is no law. ¹⁴ Nevertheless death reigned from Adam to Moses, even over them that had not sinned after the similitude of Adam's transgression, who is the figure of him that was to come.

If there were no Law – how did God judge the world before Noah? Also, God declares in the Torah that sin in ignorance is still sin and accountable to the person, and that when they discover their sin – then just measures He prescribed are to be followed. Death was caused by separation from the Tree of Life – not something as Paul describes herein. Search the Hebrew Holy Scripture and Torah and see if you can find an account that says Adam and Eve "sinned" and doomed all their offspring to depravity. Such a thought doesn't exist until Paul perverted the truth and introduced his imaginations and paganization of Christianity. Live by the words of God – search His words out to the DSS and know the truth has no part in Paul. If mankind became depraved, why did God tell Cain, after the fall: "Surely, if you improve yourself, you will be forgiven. Sin rests at the door, its desire is towards you, yet you can conquer it."

¹⁵But not as the offence, so also is the free gift. For <u>if through the offence of one</u> many be dead, much more the grace of God, and the gift by grace, which is by one man, Jesus Christ, hath abounded unto many. ¹⁶And not as it was by one that sinned, so is the gift: for the judgment was by one to condemnation, but the free gift is of many offences unto justification. ¹⁷For if by one man's offence death reigned by one; much more they which receive abundance of grace and of the gift of righteousness shall reign in life by one, Jesus Christ.)

"If" is a huge word, considering one cannot find such a teaching from Yeshua as told by his chosen emissaries, the apostles, who wrote Matthew as a collective effort well before 50 CE in Hebrew. Study out the Hebrew Gospel of Matthew at http://www.onedisciletoanother.org and see that what Paul taught here is non-existent in the account of the apostles of Jesus – who gave us Matthew in the Hebrew – and which was altered in the Greek texts. God has always had grace towards men – but He has never offered anyone vicarious atonement due to the righteousness of one being imputed to another. See what Yeshua taught – pay close attention. See what God commanded – pay close attention. See what the prophecies foretell of "that prophet" and the "one to whom rule is due" and teaching so that the Gentiles would also consider keeping the Torah or God to be honorable. Paul makes Jesus to say the words of God are a curse – which is a lie.

¹⁸Therefore as by the offence of one judgment came upon all men to condemnation; even so by the righteousness of one the free gift came upon all men unto justification of life. ¹⁹ For as by one man's disobedience many were made sinners, so by the obedience of one shall many be made righteous.

Neither of these premises from Paul are true – in fact, scripture defies them both!

Ezekiel 18 completely refutes these words of Paul.

[20]Moreover the law entered, that the offence might abound. But where sin abounded, grace did much more abound: [21]That as sin hath reigned unto death, even so might grace reign through righteousness unto eternal life by Jesus Christ our Lord.

God said He gave the Law to bless us and elevate us – to all who would make His Instruction and Decree to be their manner of life, faith, hope and trust. One Law is for all, so that all might be blessed and abide in His everlasting kindness and that He might be gracious unto all who love Him as shown through their faithfulness to the Everlasting Covenant and the Teachings from Yeshua of the Doctrine of God – as given in the Hebrew Gospel of Matthew. The Law is inseparable from the Teachings of God and Yeshua. As God said: "Choose life, that ye may live!"

Footnotes

e. Romans 5:1 Many manuscripts *let us*
f. Romans 5:2 Or *let us*
g. Romans 5:3 Or *let us*

Romans 6
Dead to Sin, Alive in Christ

⁶What shall we say then? Shall we continue in sin, that grace may abound? ²God forbid. How shall we, that are dead to sin, live any longer therein? ³Know ye not, that so many of us as were baptized into Jesus Christ were baptized into his death? ⁴Therefore we are buried with him by baptism into death: that like as Christ was raised up from the dead by the glory of the Father, even so we also should walk in newness of life.

⁵For if we have been planted together in the likeness of his death, we shall be also in the likeness of his resurrection: ⁶Knowing this, that our old man is crucified with him, that the body of sin might be destroyed, that henceforth we should not serve sin. ⁷For he that is dead is freed from sin.

⁸Now if we be dead with Christ, we believe that we shall also live with him: ⁹Knowing that Christ being raised from the dead dieth no more; death hath no more dominion over him. ¹⁰For in that he died, he died unto sin once: but in that he liveth, he liveth unto God.

¹¹Likewise reckon ye also yourselves to be dead indeed unto sin, but alive unto God through Jesus Christ our Lord. ¹²Let not sin therefore reign in your mortal body, that ye should obey it in the lusts thereof. ¹³Neither yield ye your members as instruments of unrighteousness unto sin: but yield yourselves unto God, as those that are alive from the dead, and your members as instruments of righteousness unto God. ¹⁴For sin shall not have dominion over you: for ye are not under the law, but under grace.

This chapter presents a number of false reasonings regarding sin and the role Jesus has to his disciples. In the gospel account the call is to first repent and turn to do righteousness as defined by the word of God. Recall that God has always accepted those who repent and turn to do what He declared just and right – to live reasonable lives before God and man. If this is the case – according to God and Jesus – what is this that Paul is teaching that we die when we are baptized? Jesus was baptized, and per the gospel baptism was first done by John as the baptism of repentance to then be forgiven as we then do the will of God that we neglected to do beforehand. John's teachings were remarkably simple – nothing hard to do or understand. Baptism was first given in the Law for priests to wash themselves ritually before donning their priestly garments to serve God and the people in the Temple. Some have called baptism the "outward sign of inward grace," and this might be a way to look at it. It would also be valid to view it as the time we make public profession of our faith and intent to faithfulness towards God in following in the footsteps and

teachings of Jesus, as he was also baptized to "fulfill all righteousness," that we at that time see ourselves as yoked with him in doing the will of Elohim Almighty. No where did John or Jesus or any of the Torah indicate baptism had anything to do with death or resurrection. Millions have been baptized that it clearly had no impact on their life to then do righteousness because they had died and thereafter "Christ lived within them." If we repent, we turn from doing wrong to then do what is right – and it's a growing process – not an instant remedy that imparts the righteousness of Jesus on us because he is now in us through the rite – as though it was some kind of magical rite or incantation. The heart that turns to live uprightly before God has always been precious in His sight – and doing the will of God brings His blessings, promises and kindness towards us – repentance restores our relationship to God as we then turn to follow in the footsteps of Jesus through being his disciples, just as did the twelve disciples. As Yeshua said: it is enough to be like him, but how can we be like him and pay no heed to what he said his disciples will do? Paul never teaches anything practical like explaining how his teachings find harmony with those of Jesus. Recall Paul said he was unable to keep the Law, and if this is true, according to God, such a person refuses His instruction; according to Jesus, such a person is not his disciple, as he taught his disciples to consider it honorable to keep the word and instruction of God.

Slaves to Righteousness

[15]What then? shall we sin, because we are not under the law, but under grace? God forbid. [16]Know ye not, that to whom ye yield yourselves servants to obey, his servants ye are to whom ye obey; whether of sin unto death, or of obedience unto righteousness? [17]But God be thanked, that ye were the servants of sin, but ye have obeyed from the heart that form of doctrine which was delivered you. [18]Being then made free from sin, ye became the servants of righteousness.

[19]I speak after the manner of men because of the infirmity of your flesh: for as ye have yielded your members servants to uncleanness and to iniquity unto iniquity; even so now yield your members servants to righteousness unto holiness. [20]For when ye were the servants of sin, ye were free from righteousness. [21]What fruit had ye then in those things whereof ye are now ashamed? for the end of those things is death. [22]But now being made free from sin, and become servants to God, ye have your fruit unto holiness, and the end everlasting life. [23]For the wages of sin is death; but the gift of God is eternal life through Jesus Christ our Lord.

Jesus would agree with God, that He gave His instructions to elevate us – that we know His will and not do evil. The Law is still in effect – regardless of what Paul said. The matter we've been told that it must be perfectly keeping 613 commandments has no proof in the word of God or Jesus or any true prophet of

Elohim. Neither are there Seven Noahide Laws (both laws invented by the same Rabbi more than 1000 years after Jesus). One Law is for all – one Everlasting Covenant is for all who turn to the pathways of life God desires we walk within (***Isaiah 56). God expects all His people to honor the Covenant Conditions given and ratified at Sinai. God has not set His word aside as unable to accomplish that for which it was given; to bless us, and – to see if we will do as He commanded – or not. Judgment has been decreed – Paul cannot annul a single word of God – neither can the Pope, Luther, Westly, Campbell, Joseph Smith, or Ellen White – no one can annul the word and Covenant of God, not even Paul or Billy Graham. Read Psalm 119 and see if you think the Law of God is useful as the Psalm says it is – or not. Where in Psalm 119 do we find any accord to the teachings of Paul? Is our soul restored by knowing we are doing the will of God, and thereby remaining in His sure mercies? Psalm 1 is a great and simple teaching for everyone. You may also look at Psalm 2 and consider if we are now in the time this Psalm spoke of.

Footnotes

h. Romans 6:6 Or be rendered *powerless*

i. Romans 6:23 Or *through*

Romans 7
Released from the Law, Bound to Christ

Know ye not, brethren, (for I speak to them that know the law,) how that the law hath dominion over a man as long as he liveth? ²For the woman which hath an husband is bound by the law to her husband so long as he liveth; but if the husband be dead, she is loosed from the law of her husband. ³So then if, while her husband liveth, she be married to another man, she shall be called an adulteress: but if her husband be dead, she is free from that law; so that she is no adulteress, though she be married to another man. ⁴Wherefore, my brethren, ye also are become dead to the law by the body of Christ; that ye should be married to another, even to him who is raised from the dead, that we should bring forth fruit unto God. ⁵For when we were in the flesh, the motions of sins, which were by the law, did work in our members to bring forth fruit unto death. ⁶But now we are delivered from the law, that being dead wherein we were held; that we should serve in newness of spirit.

Do you want to trust in dreams? Or reality? One is an imagination, the other is born out by reality and observable facts. One is seen, the other unseen. God revealed Himself at Sinai. God showed Yeshua approved by his Teachings, works, death and resurrection – all in accord to His word – if we but correct the false accounts and perversion of His word that were foisted upon mankind by Rome and their followers. God is not mocked, and certain judgment is decreed towards those who do the works of Satan to falsely accuse others, and who falsely accuse His good word and will towards mankind. From the first of the Ten Decrees we know that the definition of love for God has observable actions – there is no mystery of who really loves God, and anyone can easily determine who loves God by what they say about His Instructions in Righteousness and warnings to do no evil. Nothing He asks "My people" to do is too hard to hear, understand or do. So why is Paul so averse or against the Law as to say that in Christ we are freed from the Law – when Yeshua said his disciples will not even think that he came to loosen or do away with it. This is but one proof that Matthew is the only valid gospel account: the Sermon on the Mount and it's obvious ties to teach the Law, Prophets, and Psalms in almost every verse. Search the teachings of Yeshua out and you should easily see that Paul is not telling us any upright truth of God. In Paul the Law is a curse and impossible to keep. As disciples of Yeshua, we are empowered to know the Law is good and recognize those who have altered it or who speak against it are those who have made themselves enemies of God by rejecting His word and declaring what God said is good to be evil and a curse. Paul taught a

gospel of nonsense that has no part in doing the will of God or abiding in His kindness and blessing. Divisions between Churches all center from false doctrines of Paul – look at each churches Doctrinal Statements and note how many passages of support are from books in the NT written by Paul. Stop being deluded by lies against God. God has said we all belong to Him. Our eyes should be on Him first. We don't belong to each other. We should respect each other and live in equality because He alone is God and the right to "rule" belongs to him to whom it is due (Gen. 49:10). If Jesus set the rules – it is easily observed Paul is teaching AGAINST Yeshua's right to rule and inserting lies and declaring them true because he said so. Determine if you believe God – or not. Stop the pretending and imaginations of "Spiritual mysteries" and observe the plain truth of God. No one needs to be "Spiritual" to judge Paul is not teaching the observable truth of God and Jesus.

The Law and Sin

[7] What shall we say then? Is the law sin? God forbid. Nay, I had not known sin, but by the law: for I had not known lust, except the law had said, Thou shalt not covet. [8] But sin, taking occasion by the commandment, wrought in me all manner of concupiscence. For without the law sin was dead. [9] For I was alive without the law once: but when the commandment came, sin revived, and I died. [10] And the commandment, which was ordained to life, I found to be unto death. [11] For sin, taking occasion by the commandment, deceived me, and by it slew me. [12] Wherefore the law is holy, and the commandment holy, and just, and good.

Where has God said anything like this? Where has any true prophet spoken these things? Nowhere, that's where. Think back to what God told Cain. God declared Cain responsible for his own actions and that if he didn't take control of his own actions that sin would rule over him. All this passage does is let us know the true relationship Paul has with God – that sin was ruling over Paul – and this was due to his own lack of self-control – and rather than blaming himself for his own actions, Paul blames the Law of God!!! Paul interjects his nonsense of "sin deceived me" – when he is self-delusional. Do you think yourself incapable to do good because God said it was good? Do you think yourself incapable to not do an evil thing? Do you believe because the Law says to "do no evil" that all you are capable of from that moment is doing evil because God said to do no evil? Church is not a hospital for sinners – it is the assembly of called out believers to worship God in spirit and truth.

[13] Was then that which is good made death unto me? God forbid. But sin, that it might appear sin, working death in me by that which is good; that sin by the commandment might become exceeding sinful.

Paul was not dead to anyone but God and speaking the truth of God. Are the people of God to consider themselves living zombies?!? God gave the Law – His gracious instructions in righteousness – that we should become wise to reality and living a life that God can bless. As God said: "Choose life, that ye may live!" God nor Yeshua ever called anyone to be "Zombies for Jesus." Rather than spiritualizing everyone and everything, we should be observing what God and Jesus taught. Life is not about flesh versus spirit, it is that while we are living beings – body of flesh and spirit of life given by God – that we live the best life we can, and that is what the Covenant Standards are all about – so we can observe the will of God and be blessed in our coming and in our going.

[14] For we know that the law is spiritual: but I am carnal, sold under sin. [15] For that which I do I allow not: for what I would, that do I not; but what I hate, that do I. [16] If then I do that which I would not, I consent unto the law that it is good. [17] Now then it is no more I that do it, but sin that dwelleth in me. [18] For I know that in me (that is, in my flesh,) dwelleth no good thing: for to will is present with me; but how to perform that which is good I find not. [19] For the good that I would I do not: but the evil which I would not, that I do. [20] Now if I do that I would not, it is no more I that do it, but sin that dwelleth in me.

Did God sell Cain, or any man, to sin or the Serpent or Satan (accuser)? No, God said otherwise in warning Cain to not let sin rule over him! Paul is providing us all direct evidence by his words to let us know who he belonged to. Think about it very carefully. Also, God declared His word is very near to us – within our nature since we were created in His image – to become wise and like Him as humanly possible – by being taught His pathways of justice and righteousness and mercy. God has instructed just the opposite of what Paul says here – that we are sold out to sin and incapable to do good from our nature. Did God create Adam in His image – or the image of the fallen angels? (I Enoch and Genesis) In fact, Jesus taught that what comes out of the man defiles the man, not what goes into him (speaking of food). Is our heart our nature – the essence of who we are? What we do proceeds from within our nature – and we have to deny the reality being created in the image of God to pretend this nonsense of Paul. I can't speak for anyone but myself – but it isn't against me to do good to others as it is within my ability and resources to do. No – it's quite easy to do what is good. No one is perfect, but God has long ago decreed justice in the Torah whenever He decreed: "And so he shall be forgiven." It was whoever did not accept the justice of God that was to be "cut off from amongst the brethren." (Leviticus) We cannot blame our sin on sin or sinful nature – sin – defying what God said is just and good – comes from within us if we reject the gracious instruction in righteousness – and we have no one to blame but ourselves. God declared Cain responsible – and thereby gave this knowledge from

before the flood. Once again, as God said: "Choose life that ye may live!" and "Surely if you improve yourself, you will be forgiven."

²¹I find then a law, that, when I would do good, evil is present with me. ²²For I delight in the law of God after the inward man: ²³But I see another law in my members, warring against the law of my mind, and bringing me into captivity to the law of sin which is in my members. ²⁴O wretched man that I am! who shall deliver me from the body of this death? ²⁵I thank God through Jesus Christ our Lord. So then with the mind I myself serve the law of God; but with the flesh the law of sin.

Yes, Paul was a wretched man. Don't judge me for saying this, as I'm just agreeing with his own assessment of himself. He spoke honestly when giving us that information! We all make decisions in life. We've all been lied to when the writings of Paul were put into the Bible and New Testament. As one passage tells of the Gentiles – we have inherited lies. Rather than believe the apostle who lies against God – we should choose to abide in the words of Almighty God and the prophet who taught that it is honorable to keep the Instructions of God in the Torah (Isaiah 42). God did not create Adam to be a slave, but a free man – to rule over and subdue the earth. As Yeshua said, he is the Christ – and all of us – including the Apostles, are brethren – not rulers or slaves. Study the Ten Decrees – they are also based on equality.

Jeremiah 16:19

"O LORD, my strength, and my fortress, and my refuge in the day of affliction, the Gentiles shall come unto thee from the ends of the earth, and shall say, **Surely our fathers have inherited lies, vanity, and wherein *is* no profit."**

Surely, this is because none of the Roman or Protestant reformers bothered to follow the words of God to make sure writings they put in the New Testament were in accord with the words of God, as were the Teachings of Yeshua (Jesus). (Deut. 4, 12, 13, 18)

Footnotes

h. Romans 7:5 In contexts like this, the Greek word for flesh (sarx) refers to the sinful state of human beings, often presented as a power in opposition to the Spirit.

i. Romans 7:7 Exodus 20:17; Deut. 5:21

j. Romans 7:18 Or *my flesh*

k. Romans 7:25 Or *in the flesh*

Romans 8
Life through the Spirit

⁸There is therefore now no condemnation to them which are in Christ Jesus, who walk not after the flesh, but after the Spirit. ²For the law of the Spirit of life in Christ Jesus hath made me free from the law of sin and death. ³For what the law could not do, in that it was weak through the flesh, God sending his own Son in the likeness of sinful flesh, and for sin, condemned sin in the flesh: ⁴That the righteousness of the law might be fulfilled in us, who walk not after the flesh, but after the Spirit.

To be a faithful disciple requires making the Covenant and the Teachings (Doctrine of God) as taught by Jesus to be our guide and manner of life. If we are faithful to the words of God – doing His will is our righteousness – and it is of Him, as they are His instructions, not of ourselves. What we do is agree with God's standards as we do them. We reform our conscience to be in alignment to His instruction. It is His word that sanctifies us – that sets us apart to Him. It is His word that is truth. It is His will that we seek to do and grow in producing the fruit He desires in our lives as we mature. When we do good – what is found wanting when we trust in His provisions and opportunities in life? We look to do good, we spurn evil and association with those who are evil. There is no evil in the Instructions of God as given at Sinai – only hope, trust and knowing good from evil, or secular from holy. As we do His good will, we allow His Spirit to write His instruction on our hearts that we do them from our heart. Nothing required of the "Spirit" to understand any "mysteries", as God has fully revealed both Himself and His will and His plans towards those who do His will to be very different from those who refuse or reject His instruction. All the Instructions of God can be observed – we can also observe those who make the claim to be a Christian and who don't have the proof James spoke of, that he can show his faith by his works.

Carefully read Matthew, especially the Hebrew Gospel of Matthew. Where in all his teachings or the prophecies noted did Yeshua or the Prophets foretell Yeshua was to be a blood sacrifice for the sins of the world as Paul said? I have yet to find it. The passages from Isaiah 53 don't make this claim. Go back to the Dead Sea Scrolls and the Jewish Holy Scripture – read their study editions, such as the 14 volume set from Soncino – many are the claims Christians make for passages that are taken out of context or are mistranslated or altered in the Greek. In the sermon of Peter on Pentecost in Acts the point is made that Jesus came to turn us from our iniquities – NOT to excuse our iniquity and promote Torahless living as taught by

Paul. We may pretend all our lives – but one day each of us will give account to God. Will we be able to do so by the words of a false apostle? I'd rather do my best to honor the word of God.

⁵For they that are after the flesh do mind the things of the flesh; but they that are after the Spirit the things of the Spirit. ⁶For to be carnally minded is death; but to be spiritually minded is life and peace. ⁷Because the carnal mind is enmity against God: for it is not subject to the law of God, neither indeed can be. ⁸So then they that are in the flesh cannot please God.

These words from Paul prove he was incorporating pagan ideas into Christianity. Man is a living soul, and our flesh is not the cause of sin. The "Spirit" doesn't magically impart the words of God apart from His word. The Spirit works with the word, just as told in the Creation account of Genesis. Paul is great evidence to prove the point! Paul consulted no man to know his gospel – he received it by "revelation" and not by any man, which includes Jesus. There is no accord with the "gospel" of "revelation of Jesus Christ" received by Paul to the Teachings of Jesus. There is no accord in the accounts from Paul of the Law or Jewish history that find accord to any sound principle or any True Instruction of God or knowledge of His will or Torah – abject ignorance is all Paul was capable of by his "Spirit" and "revelation". God is not the author of confusion. The truth is simple – as with Cain, so with us: If we repent to do rightly (live according to the instructions of God – every word of God – not currently practiced "cut and paste" options) God will forgive us and elevate us and we can abide in His presence, promises and kindness. Life brings many tests of our faith – each of us is on an individual journey – but we must agree that we will do our best and get up when we trip or fall and continue on in His pathway and do no evil. As told in Exodus, God allows trials to come our way to see if we will obey Him – or not. Trust in God. God is good. His words of life are everlasting and true. "Thy word is truth" Even the gospel of John claims "Sanctify them by Thy truth; Thy word is truth."

⁹But ye are not in the flesh, but in the Spirit, if so be that the Spirit of God dwell in you. Now if any man have not the Spirit of Christ, he is none of his. ¹⁰And if Christ be in you, the body is dead because of sin; but the Spirit is life because of righteousness. ¹¹But if the Spirit of him that raised up Jesus from the dead dwell in you, he that raised up Christ from the dead shall also quicken your mortal bodies by his Spirit that dwelleth in you.

God gives of His Spirit to write His Teachings in our heart to help us keep His pathways in life (Ezekiel 37), this is not the same as rejecting the Law as unable to do that for which God gave it. Is Paul declaring God unfaithful and ignorant? So long as our neighbors can see us, we are not "in the Spirit." Paul sounds more like a deluded mad man than someone who knows enough that we

should listen to him. Who put Paul into our Bibles? Not God. God gives life. There is not a "Trinity" – there is but One God we are to serve – God said so, the Prophets and Psalms say so; and Jesus definitely said so. Trinity was developed hundreds of years after Jesus and the Apostles. Trinity is a pagan belief system – and is found nowhere in the Holy Scripture. All will be resurrected – some to receive their rewards from God as due – some to everlasting condemnation – as due. Since all are to be resurrected to face God and give account for themselves – does the Spirit also dwell in the enemies of God as in the faithful? Hardly. Paul was a poor religion inventor – he makes no sense at all and consistently twists or denies the words of God. It's no wonder Paul is at the center of all Church divisions.

[12]Therefore, brethren, we are debtors, not to the flesh, to live after the flesh. [13]For if ye live after the flesh, ye shall die: but if ye through the Spirit do mortify the deeds of the body, ye shall live.

Are we incapable to resist sin or evil? Must we do evil the more we know the manner of life that God desires we live if we call upon His NAME? Hardly so. I know many people who will have nothing to do with institutional religion that are among the most moral and just I've ever met – and they don't pretend to live by "the Spirit", but according to their conscience – and they don't want to treat others unfairly. Fact is that much evil is done by those who claim to be "Christians", as well as some in Zionist Orthodox Judaism. In fact, child predators are adept to search out Churches to accept them as they groom their victims. Words are cheap. There is no accord in the Pauline gospel of cheap grace to the Grace God has declared towards those who honor and keep His word faithfully. If God is the Creator who created Adam in His image, if God created the heavens and the earth – our obligation is to Him by learning the pathway of life He said to live in: "The Holy Way." Recall that the Mercy Seat of the Covenant covers the Covenant – which might be seen as saying the mercy of God covers those who make those Covenant Standards their Standards to live by.

[14]For those who are led by the Spirit of God are the children of God. [15]The Spirit you received does not make you slaves, so that you live in fear again; rather, the Spirit you received brought about your adoption to sonship.[f] And by him we cry, *"Abba,*[g] Father." [16]The Spirit himself testifies with our spirit that we are God's children. [17]Now if we are children, then we are heirs—heirs of God and co-heirs with Christ, if indeed we share in his sufferings in order that we may also share in his glory.

Rather we share in the work of Jesus – that we take his yoke upon us and learn from him. Being yoked to Jesus is to work along-side of him – not to ride on his

back as a freeloader. Through discipleship to Jesus, we are freed to obey God, rather than man or man-made imaginations that defy the Instructions of God.

Present Suffering and Future Glory

¹⁸For I reckon that the sufferings of this present time are not worthy to be compared with the glory which shall be revealed in us. ¹⁹For the earnest expectation of the creature waiteth for the manifestation of the sons of God. ²⁰For the creature was made subject to vanity, not willingly, but by reason of him who hath subjected the same in hope, ²¹Because the creature itself also shall be delivered from the bondage of corruption into the glorious liberty of the children of God.

God's children can be observed by their living as He instructed all men to live. This is why Jesus said that men should see our works as good, that God be praised. Jesus also said one doesn't light a candle and put it under a bushel, but it is lit and set in place that it provides light to all in the house – so it is with being able to observe who the children of God are – and who is not, but say they are. God called Israel His son. The unique prophet to come, Jesus (Joshua), was known as the "son of God" in the same sense, but in a unique and provable role. No other Jew in all human history has been praised and honored above other men as is Jesus – even though the accounts have been altered, millions point to the Sermon on the Mount as perhaps the best teaching given in all human history. Also, the angels were called "the sons of God." Yet both are spoken of in Scripture to have been created by God – not birthed by God as a physical descendant. Perhaps the Psalms of David give the best evidence of the hope of those whose trust is in God for all things.

²²For we know that the whole creation groaned and travailed in pain together until now. ²³And not only they, but ourselves also, which have the first fruits of the Spirit, even we ourselves groan within ourselves, waiting for the adoption, to wit, the redemption of our body. ²⁴For we are saved by hope: but hope that is seen is not hope: for what a man seethe, why doth he yet hope for? ²⁵But if we hope for that we see not, then do we with patience wait for it.

"For we know that the whole creation groaneth and travaileth in pain together until now"? **Where do we learn this? I can find no other witness to this being fact in the Holy Scripture or the Teachings of Jesus. How can we know what Paul said we all know, when we don't know, and we can't prove it either? No, I don't know – and given the limited view of the "whole creation" in Paul's day, let alone in our day with the aid of the Hubble Telescope – it is quite unknowable – common sense should cause us to pause and evaluate the claims Paul made – who are the witnesses that prove him true? I have yet to fine just one – let alone two or more, as God** commanded. Recall Isaiah's words: "If they speak not according to the Law and the Testimony, there is no light in them." It would be extremely presumptuous to think in all the Universe that Earth is the only inhabited planet where God created life. How could a just God hold the entire Universe guilty or in bondage because of our problem? It is not hard to grasp that God will hold each person accountable for their own actions – not placing their blame on others. The only exception to this in the Covenant has to do with generational curse when one gives false testimony in the NAME of God to deceive – and if our eyes are open, we can easily observe this today in how some get farther and farther from living as He said we are to live, and who deliberately teach both their children and others to obey them, rather than the stated will of God. Use your brains – not your feelings that have been so easily manipulated. Who upholds the Covenant Standards to observe to do them because they are good and because they are obviously reasonable, and reportedly given by the God who created humans in His image!? None of those decrees lead anyone to sin – cause them to sin - and those who claim that they do have no knowledge and no root in themselves.

Also, our hope remains for what God has in store in the restoration, when all things are made new. What we do on earth – does it bind all creation to our fate from disbelief of the words of God? There is no need to think God not capable to have populated unknown number of planets, and it is likely that not all refused to believe what He said is true. Say a race in a universe beyond our sight were to sin and then God bound upon us their due penalty – would God be just and true to His word to hold the one who sins accountable, and that the righteous will not be held accountable for the sins of the wicked? I can't think of a reason in the world why I need to believe anything Paul wrote – let alone the forgeries that pretend his authorship. Scholarship knows some books attributed to him are forgeries. Paul's biggest disciple set out to recover all of Paul's books about 100 CE – Marcion – and he was the first heretic, denying the gospels and inventing his own version of Luke. Marcion had 10 of Paul's writings – where did we get the rest?

Regarding "hope" – and what is "unseen" – this common theme of Paul about what cannot be seen, the invisible – is opposed to the directions given by God and Jesus, that we need to be knowledgeable and observant of what we are doing, as well as the need to observe if others are in need that we are able to help. As one Prophet summed it up: "What does God require of you, O man, but to live justly, love mercy, and walk humbly with thy God." Jesus taught likewise.

[26]Likewise the Spirit also helped our infirmities: for we know not what we should pray for as we ought: but the Spirit itself maketh intercession for us with groanings which cannot be uttered. [27]And he that searched the hearts knoweth what is the mind of the Spirit, because

he maketh intercession for the saints according to the will of God. ²⁸And we know that all things work together for good to them that love God, to them who are the called according to his purpose. ²⁹For whom he did foreknow, he also did predestinate to be conformed to the image of his Son, that he might be the firstborn among many brethren. ³⁰Moreover whom he did predestinate, them he also called: and whom he called, them he also justified: and whom he justified, them he also glorified.

Matthew 20:14 and 22:16 both have Jesus teaching that "many are called, but few are chosen." Romans 8:30 is one of the divisive verses in the NT, as it testifies against these passages from Jesus in Matthew – formally known as the doctrine of predestination – the passages in Matthew prove Paul to have provided testimony against the Teachings of Jesus. Study Bible editions quite often support the teachings of Paul via other places where Paul wrote similar teachings of his gospel. Is it curious that the on-line edition for the KJV made no mention of this teaching of Jesus that relates directly to verse 30. It only proves what I'm bringing up is a problem. God gave standards of testimony or witness. We need to evaluate the writings of Paul by the words of God – not the rantings and imaginations of a man who defied the Doctrine and Law of God and the teachings of Jesus.

More Than Conquerors

³¹What shall we then say to these things? If God be for us, who can be against us? ³²He that spared not his own Son, but delivered him up for us all, how shall he not with him also freely give us all things? ³³Who shall lay anything to the charge of God's elect? It is God that justifieth. ³⁴Who is he that condemned? It is Christ that died, yea rather, that is risen again, who is even at the right hand of God, who also maketh intercession for us. ³⁵Who shall separate us from the love of Christ? shall tribulation, or distress, or persecution, or famine, or nakedness, or peril, or sword? ³⁶As it is written, For thy sake we are killed all the day long; we are accounted as sheep for the slaughter. ³⁷Nay, in all these things we are more than conquerors through him that loved us. ³⁸For I am persuaded, that neither death, nor life, nor angels, nor principalities, nor powers, nor things present, nor things to come, ³⁹Nor height, nor depth, nor any other creature, shall be able to separate us from the love of God, which is in Christ Jesus our Lord.

Better to believe God than any man. According to God, what brings us closer to God – elevates us? Keeping His commandments as our Standard and rule of life and conduct. How did He say to do this? By observing His teachings in the Covenant Standards to do them – not by believing hard enough, or faithing hard enough – but by observing what He decreed and making those Standards to be our Standards to live by. That is not hard to understand, so why does Paul in his writing teach otherwise??

What separates us from God? Go back and read the Ten Decrees given by God at Sinai – those who reject His word and testify falsely of Him to deceive are those who are cursed. If this is wrongly understood – I'm open to learning from those with better understanding – but it must be proven by the words of God. If you think God promised what Paul said in Romans 8 – you'd better go back and see what God said. While you are at it, see if Jesus taught likewise in Matthew.

All things do work for the good of those that love God. The stories of faithful saints in the Bible repeatedly tell us this – such as Joseph saying to his brothers: "You meant it for evil, but God used it for good." God defined love in the First decree to be those who love Him AND keep His commandments. If you believe otherwise – talk to God about it – read the Torah and see what God had to say – with the focus to do as Yeshua instructed: "Man shall not live by bread alone, but by every word that proceeds from the mouth of God." According to God, love is known by what it does. From my personal observed view, the Decrees all give profound definition to what love is – <u>and what it is not</u>.

This must also be said because of the rantings of Paul: Who did God say He will reject? Did God ever say such a thing? I wonder if it is a form of "whoredom" to run after those who defame what God has blessed? If God judged Israel for the same thing – long ago – are we wise to think God would defy His justice?

Hosea 4: Hear the word of the Lord, ye children of Israel: for the Lord hath a controversy with the inhabitants of the land, because there is no truth, nor mercy, nor knowledge of God in the land. ²By swearing, and lying, and killing, and stealing, and committing adultery, they break out, and blood touched blood. ³Therefore shall the land mourn, and everyone that dwelleth therein shall languish, with the beasts of the field, and with the fowls of heaven; yea, the fishes of the sea also shall be taken away. ⁴Yet let no man strive, nor reprove another: for thy people are as they that strive with the priest. ⁵Therefore shalt thou fall in the day, and the prophet also shall fall with thee in the night, and I will destroy thy mother. ⁶**<u>My people are destroyed for lack of knowledge: because thou hast rejected knowledge, I will also reject thee</u>**, that thou shalt be no priest to me: seeing thou hast forgotten the law of thy God, I will also forget thy children. ⁷As they were increased, so they sinned against me: therefore, will I change their glory into shame. ⁸They eat up the sin of my people, and they set their heart on their iniquity. ⁹And there shall be, like people, like priest: and I will punish them for their ways and reward them their doings. ¹⁰For they shall eat, and not have enough: they shall commit whoredom, and shall not increase: because they have left off to take heed to the Lord. ¹¹Whoredom and wine and new wine take away the heart. ¹²My people ask counsel at their stocks, and their staff declared unto them: for the spirit of whoredoms hath caused them to err, and they have gone a whoring from under their God.

Footnotes

n. Romans 8:2 The Greek is singular; some manuscripts *me*

o. Romans 8:3 In contexts like this, the Greek word for flesh *(sarx)* refers to the sinful state of human beings, often presented as a power in opposition to the Spirit; also in verses 4-13.

p. Romans 8:3 Or *flesh, for sin*

q. Romans 8:10 Or *you, your body is dead because of sin, yet your spirit is alive*

r. Romans 8:11 Some manuscripts *bodies through*

s. Romans 8:15 The Greek word for adoption to sonship is a term referring to the full legal standing of an adopted male heir in Roman culture; also in verse 23.

t. Romans 8:15 Aramaic for father

u. Romans 8:21 Or *subjected it in hope.* ²¹For

v. Romans 8:28 Or *that all things work together for good to those who love God, who;* or *that in all things God works together with those who love him to bring about what is good—with those who*

w. Romans 8:36 Psalm 44:22

x. Romans 8:38 Or *nor heavenly rulers*

Romans 9
Paul's Anguish Over Israel

⁹I say the truth in Christ, I lie not, my conscience also bearing me witness in the Holy Ghost, ²That I have great heaviness and continual sorrow in my heart. ³For I could wish that myself were accursed from Christ for my brethren, my kinsmen according to the flesh: ⁴Who are Israelites; to whom pertaineth the adoption, and the glory, and the covenants, and the giving of the law, and the service of God, and the promises; ⁵Whose are the fathers, and of whom as concerning the flesh Christ came, who is over all, God blessed forever. Amen.

According to early Christian history, Paul was completing a vow at the Temple to prove repentance or absolution of the charges against him. Read Acts 20 – 23, as it is a book written to foster belief in Paul. Were the charges against him to have been teaching Jews (Jewish disciples of Jesus) that they no longer needed to keep the Law and Covenant as given by God? Acts says Paul voluntarily submitted to the vow and paid for the witnesses to be present in the Temple with him in an attempt to be absolved of the charges. An uproar resulted near the end, due to one of Paul's supposed disciples defiling the Temple. Anyone can read his writings and know the charges made against him were justly charged, as we have adequate evidence in the writings of his books in the New Testament. The charges against Paul in the Damascus Documents of antiquity found in the Dead Sea Scrolls are of one who was charged to be a liar, and the connection is too obvious to pretend to ignore or not directly suspect Paul. Given the anti-Law teachings of Paul we have in the records of his writings in the New Testament, given the words of God in the rest of our Bible, given the teachings of Jesus in Matthew – no Church authority or Bible Publisher should have put a single writing of Paul into the same book and then tell anyone it is the "inerrant word of God." Up to this point it has been shown that what Paul was writing is not in accord to the Teachings of God up through Jesus' teaching ministry. Because Paul says: "1I speak the truth in Christ—I am not lying, my conscience confirms it through the Holy Spirit," the matter is his conscience is not a valid witness to truth. The word of God is a valid witness to truth. The "multitude of believers" who complained to the apostles of Paul teaching contrary doctrines might be considered a valid witness, as they all testified to what Paul was teaching – and we can review the writings of Paul and observe the charges made were true – Paul was teaching against the Law – and the Teachings of Jesus in the account written by his chosen disciples, the twelve apostles, we know Jesus said to live by every word that proceeds from the mouth

of God – and the Bible centers around those spoken at Mount Sinai and which were then written on stone tablets and placed in the Ark of the Covenant.

God gave standards of witness for trials in the Torah. No where in all the Holy Scripture is one person claiming he hasn't violated his conscience a valid standard of testimony of fact. We can all have our own opinions and do things that don't matter much, but to testify against God and call His Everlasting Covenant to have been done away with on the cross – at variance with the word of God and the Teachings of "that prophet", Jesus – these are VERY serious charges indeed. Yet we have Paul call to witness his conscience and then claim the Spirit of God testifies against the Word of God – if the gospel taught by Paul is true? It should be obvious that such a person is not to be trusted. No wonder Paul's exclamation that "I am not lying." As the old television show, Dragnet, said: "Just the facts mam – just give me the facts." The fact is that Paul in every way lied about God, the Covenant, the Doctrine of God and the Teachings of Jesus. No where in Matthew can a hint of the doctrines of Paul be found – yet he claims he is testifying that "his gospel" is true – and God and Jesus gave it to him by revelation?!! Funny that God proved to me that Paul is nothing but a rank liar – even though I used to believe him faithfully as I was taught to do – until I discovered the Teachings of Jesus and their harmony to the entire Holy Scripture and Dead Sea Scrolls – and the evidence that our Bibles were altered by Judaism and Rome – who have little to do with God or those who are faithful to His instructions – except their pretensions. (See definition of Judaism – centers from Rabbinical opinions and interpretations of scripture

Where in the Hebrew Gospel of Matthew does Jesus say he is God? Where in the Holy Scripture is there a prophecy that God will manifest Himself in human flesh and sacrifice Himself for the sins of the world? Nowhere. Does Paul end this paragraph saying Jesus is God? If so, this is a violation of the first commandment as well, as the current MT literal translation is "thou shalt not put another god on My face." God is God. Jesus prayed to God when giving the "Lord's Prayer." Was he praying to Himself?! No, he wasn't, and he never claimed to be God, but a man, a man who was to ascend to the throne on the right hand of the Power on High – the Ancient of Days in Daniel.

God's Sovereign Choice

⁶Not as though the word of God hath taken none effect. For they are not all Israel, which are of Israel: ⁷Neither, because they are the seed of Abraham, are they all children: but, In Isaac shall thy seed be called. ⁸That is, They which are the children of the flesh, these are

not the children of God: but the children of the promise are counted for the seed. ⁹For this is the word of promise, At this time will I come, and Sarah shall have a son.

⁷Who is a descendant but one who begotten through direct lineage? The matter of Abraham having a descendant was the issue in Genesis 15 – that he have an heir to inherit his property, rather than his employee inheriting it? God promised Abraham that he would have a descendant for his inheritance – even though Sarah was barren – that she would have a child – not that Abraham and Sarah having a child through the handmaid of Sarah to be the descendant of the Land promise. Genesis 16 proves the point that the heir would be from Sarah, not the handmade – it would be proven that God would be true to His word, and although both Abraham and Sarah were beyond normal childbearing age – God would be true and do that which was humanly impossible. The conflict between the offspring – Isaac and Ishmael – because of the dishonor of Isaac by Ishmael, he and Hagar were not to dwell with the child of the promise – and although given a separate promise from the angel of God – the two are descendants of Abraham – physical descendants – not imagined descendants – are separate nations to this day. For God's sake, and the sake of the world as a whole, just rest in the promises and word of God – not on fear! The children of the Promise are the children of the promise, but both were of the offspring of Abraham – both were not offspring through Abraham and Sarah. How is it as Paul says: "In other words it is not the children by physical descent who are God's children, but it is the children of the promise who are regarded as Abraham's offspring?" Abrahams wife was Sarah – and the promises were made to Abraham and his descendants – and a different promise was made to the offspring of Abraham and Hagar – and both promises are of God, but only through Sarah and Abraham would come the fulfillment of the descendants who would inherit Canaan and receive the Ten Decrees at Sinai – the Everlasting Covenant which would be a blessing to all nations – whosoever would honor the Decree and Covenant given by God Himself – not though and angel or elemental. Also of note is the fact that in later history, after Israels rejecting living as God told them to – He effectively divorced Israel when she became His enemy. The principle is basic, as told by Joshua upon entering the Land and renewing the Covenant, his words to the angel were: "Are you for us, or for those who are against us?" Are we for doing the will of God, as He gave it – or are we against it?

¹⁰Not only that, but Rebekah's children were conceived at the same time by our father Isaac. ¹¹Yet, before the twins were born or had done anything good or bad—in order that <u>God's purpose in election</u> might stand: ¹²<u>not by works</u> but by him who calls—she was told, "The older will serve the younger."[d] ¹³Just as it is written: "Jacob I loved, but Esau I hated."[e]

God knows our future, we don't. We have to live life to know what we are really going to do. God foreknew what Esau was going to do – that he would count the promised blessing of God as no more valuable than a bowl of stew. I would count that as disregarding the promises of God, and cause for the statement. It was not that God elected Esau to be who he became, or that Jacob was that good either – as one can note the story of when God changed his name to Israel – only after not being friends with idol worshippers.

Where in the words of God in the Torah does He give us information about "election"? God obviously foreknew Jacob and Esau – He is the one who forms the soul within each of us before we are born – it is the soul that either accepts or rejects God – it is the soul of a man that decides to honor God – or not. God was proving Himself to Isaac and Rebecah – that He knows who we will become before we are born. Our actions and decisions prove who we are – He foreknows – but we don't – that's because He is God and we are not. Where did God ever say it was about "election"??? God has decreed who He will have mercy on, and who He will not – and His words about this are as true today as any of His word to Adam, Cain, Noah, Abraham, Isaac, Jacob, Moses or Yeshua. This is why we need to go back and rid the Bible of false apostles writings and alterations and mistranslations to the pre-existing word given in the Hebrew Holy Scripture and the ancient records of the Dead Sea Scrolls – the Scripture of Yeshua's days on earth. God declared who He will have mercy on, and who are His enemies – in the very first of the Ten Decrees. To deny this is to deny the most important commandment/decree God gave – believe God, choose life, and live it according to His gracious instructions in righteousness!!

[14]What shall we say then? Is there unrighteousness with God? God forbid. [15]For he saith to Moses, I will have mercy on whom I will have mercy, and I will have compassion on whom I will have compassion. [16]So then it is not of him that willet, nor of him that rennet, but of God that sheweth mercy. [17]For the scripture saith unto Pharaoh, Even for this same purpose have I raised thee up, that I might shew my power in thee, and that my name might be declared throughout all the earth. [18]Therefore hath he mercy on whom he will have mercy, and whom he will he hardened.

[19]Thou wilt say then unto me, why doth he yet finds fault? For whom hath resisted his will? [20] Nay but, O man, who art thou that replies against God? Shall the thing formed say to him that formed it, why hast thou made me thus? [21] Hath not the potter power over the clay, of the same lump to make one vessel unto honor, and another unto dishonor?

Is it the will of God that anyone perish? He said His will is that all would come to the knowledge of Him and repent, that He might save them. He will be true to His word, and His word is just and righteous. Do we have the ability to reject the word

of God? Do we have the ability to observe the words of God? Are we inclined to seek out His will that we might do it? Are we inclined to double check what someone claims God said, so we can know if they speak according to His word – or not? This is a time of great deception on earth – particularly in Western society. Look at how the MSM has been foisting false charges to blind men from observing facts – to then rule by false accusation – certainly a work of those who rebel against God and seek to destroy what good remains! God hates those who sow discord among brethren, but He doesn't hate those who dare declare His word eternally true. Isaiah 30:18; "Therefore the LORD will wait, that He may be gracious to you; and therefore He will be exalted, that He may have mercy on you. For the LORD is a God of justice; blessed are all those who wait for Him."

As you read this next passage, recall that Elohim gave the "Law" – the "Covenant" to everyone the same day, and everyone present ratified it the same day – the "Law", from the beginning, was given to all – "Jew and Gentile." The same Covenant was renewed by Joshua as they all entered the "Land" together.

[NIV] 22What if God, although choosing to show his wrath and make his power known, bore with great patience the objects of his wrath—prepared for destruction? 23What if he did this to make the riches of his glory known to the objects of his mercy, whom he prepared in advance for glory— 24even us, whom he also called, not only from the Jews but also from the Gentiles? 25As he says in Hosea:

"I will call them 'my people' who are not my people; and I will call her 'my loved one' who is not my loved one,"[i]26and, "In the very place where it was said to them, 'You are not my people, 'there they will be called 'children of the living God.'"[j]

27Isaiah cries out concerning Israel: "Though the number of the Israelites be like the sand by the sea, only the remnant will be saved. 28For the Lord will carry out his sentence on earth with speed and finality."[k]

29It is just as Isaiah said previously: "Unless the Lord Almighty had left us descendants, we would have become like Sodom, we would have been like Gomorrah."[l]

Well, if Paul knew much about Isaiah he would have sited Isaiah 56 declaring those of any nation – anyone who serves Elohim alone as God, keeps His Sabbath, and who grasps His Covenant tightly – will be accepted and blessed by Him. Is the Covenant "Law" about what we do? Is what we do a "work"? or "faith". The book of James puts it nicely: "I will show you my faith by my works." It is by "faith" that we believe God is a righteous Judge that we take this seriously and seek to live in "the holy way" taught by Jesus.

Israel's Unbelief

[NIV] ³⁰What then shall we say? That the Gentiles, who did not pursue righteousness, have obtained it, a righteousness that is by faith; ³¹but the people of Israel, who pursued the law as the way of righteousness, have not attained their goal. ³²Why not? Because they pursued it not by faith but as if it were by works. They stumbled over the stumbling stone. ³³As it is written: "See, I lay in Zion a stone that causes people to stumble and a rock that makes them fall, and the one who believes in him will never be put to shame."

Read Isaiah 56. No matter whether Jew or Gentile – it's the same Standards – those given by God Himself – not some lowly angel.

Read the passages in Isaiah as noted, but this is the Hebrew Scripture for 28:16,

"Therefore, hear the word of HASHEM, O scoffing men, O rulers of this people who are in Jerusalem. For you say, "We has sealed a covenant with Death and made a compact with the Grave; when the surging staff of punishment passers through it will not come to us, for <u>we have made Deceit our shelter and taken refuge in Falsehood.</u>" Therefore, thus said my Lord HASHEM/ELOHIM: Behold, I am laying a stone for a foundation in Zion; a sturdy stone, a precious cornerstone, as secure foundation. Let the believer not expect it soon. I shall use judgment as a measuring line, and righteousness as a plumb bob<u>. Hail will sweep away the shelter of Deceit, and water will wash away the refuge of Falsehood. And your covenant with Death will be annulled, and your compact with the Grave will not be binding; when the surging staff passes through, it will pass through every morning, by day and by night; understanding of this report will being them horror."</u> Where is: "and the one who believes in him will never be put to shame?" Yeshua's teachings certainly include the judgment and righteousness God commanded of "My people." Where is judgment in the writings of Paul if he said the love of God is unconditional, yet in the first of the Ten Decrees – love, according to God IS CONDITIONAL – the condition being the Ten Decrees – just as said in Deuteronomy by God Himself! All through the Teachings of Yeshua in Matthew the references kept going to those who honor the Covenant by their faithfulness to it. It is God given standards for justice and righteousness. Would it be deceitful to say God will not use them to judge those who speak falsely against the Decrees of God and that each of us should be capable and responsible to repent – <u>that we do them and do no evil?</u> Does Paul uphold the Law as everlasting true standards of God that each of us is capable to hear, observe, and do?

Anyone who has read Matthew has to admit Yeshua taught doing the works of God. He was careful to say his disciples are to live by every word of God. The Ten Decrees are amongst the words of God, and in fact the words that God said

will be used as His rule in judgment of Jew and Gentile. God also spoke through Moses to say He would raise up a prophet from amongst Israel that whoever would not hear whatever he said to do would be "cut-off." If Yeshua (Jesus) is that prophet – and there exists very good evidence that he is in the Hebrew Gospel of Matthew – then since Yeshua said we are not to even think he came to loosen or set the Law aside – if we believe Yeshua – we cannot believe the claims of Paul, because Paul defies doing the Covenant Law and teaches it is not even given by God in Galatians 3 and 4. Be it known that the Sermon on the Mount – and other passages – are altered in the Greek version. See the link to the Hebrew Gospel of Matthew, and consider if it is the best account for us today.

http://onedscipletoanother.org/id6.html

Deuteronomy 18: 17-22; The Lord said to me: "What they say is good. I will raise up for them a prophet like you from among their fellow Israelites, and I will put my words in his mouth. He will tell them everything I commend him. I myself will call to account anyone who does not listen to my words that the prophet speaks in my name. But a prophet who presumes to speak in my name anything I have not commanded, or a prophet who speaks in the name of other gods, is to be put to death."

You may say to yourselves, "How can we know when a message has not been spoken by the Lord?" If what a prophet proclaims in the name of the Lord does not take place or come true, that is a message the Lord has not spoken. That prophet has spoken presumptuously, so do not be alarmed.

Deuteronomy 4

[1]Now, Israel, hear the decrees and laws I am about to teach you. Follow them so that you may live and may go in and take possession of the land the Lord, the God of your ancestors, is giving you. [2]Do not add to what I command you and do not subtract from it but keep the commands of the Lord your God that I give you.

[3]You saw with your own eyes what the Lord did at Baal Peor. The Lord your God destroyed from among you everyone who followed the Baal of Peor, [4]but all of you who held fast to the Lord your God are still alive today.

[5]See, I have taught you decrees and laws as the Lord my God commanded me, so that you may follow them in the land you are entering to take possession of it. [6]Observe them carefully, for this will show your wisdom and understanding to the nations, who will hear about all these decrees and say, "Surely this great nation is a wise and understanding people." [7]What other nation is so great as to have their gods near them the way the Lord our God is near us whenever we pray

to him? ⁸And what other nation is so great as to have such righteous decrees and laws as this body of laws I am setting before you today?

⁹Only be careful and watch yourselves closely so that you do not forget the things your eyes have seen or let them fade from your heart as long as you live. Teach them to your children and to their children after them. ¹⁰Remember the day you stood before the Lord your God at Horeb, when he said to me, "Assemble the people before me to hear my words so that they may learn to revere me as long as they live in the land and may teach them to their children." ¹¹You came near and stood at the foot of the mountain while it blazed with fire to the very heavens, with black clouds and deep darkness. ¹²Then the Lord spoke to you out of the fire. You heard the sound of words but saw no form; there was only a voice. ¹³He declared to you his covenant, the Ten Commandments, which he commanded you to follow and then wrote them on two stone tablets. ¹⁴And the Lord directed me at that time to teach you the decrees and laws you are to follow in the land that you are crossing the Jordan to possess.

Deuteronomy 12

²⁹The Lord your God will cut off before you the nations you are about to invade and dispossess. But when you have driven them out and settled in their land, ³⁰and after they have been destroyed before you, be careful not to be ensnared by inquiring about their gods, saying, "How do these nations serve their gods? We will do the same." ³¹You must not worship the Lord your God in their way, because in worshiping their gods, they do all kinds of detestable things the Lord hates. They even burn their sons and daughters in the fire as sacrifices to their gods.

³²See that you do all I command you; do not add to it or take away from it.

Deuteronomy 13

Worshiping Other Gods ¹[a]If a prophet, or one who foretells by dreams, appears among you and announces to you a sign or wonder, ²and if the sign or wonder spoken of takes place, and the prophet says, "Let us follow other gods" (gods you have not known) "and let us worship them," ³you must not listen to the words of that prophet or dreamer. (Yeshua never claimed to be God or co-Creator) The Lord your God is testing you to find out whether you love him with all your heart and with all your soul. ⁴It is the Lord your God you must follow, and him you must revere. Keep his commands and obey him; serve him and hold fast to him. (Yeshua taught his disciples to keep the commandments of God).

Footnotes

- y. Romans 9:5 Or *Messiah, who is over all. God be forever praised! Or Messiah. God who is over all be forever praised!*
- z. Romans 9:7 Gen. 21:12
- aa. Romans 9:9 Gen. 18:10,14
- bb. Romans 9:12 Gen. 25:23
- cc. Romans 9:13 Mal. 1:2,3
- dd. Romans 9:15 Exodus 33:19
- ee. Romans 9:17 Exodus 9:16
- ff. Romans 9:20 Isaiah 29:16; 45:9
- gg. Romans 9:25 Hosea 2:23
- hh. Romans 9:26 Hosea 1:10
- ii. Romans 9:28 Isaiah 10:22,23 (see Septuagint)
- jj. Romans 9:29 Isaiah 1:9
- kk. Romans 9:33 Isaiah 8:14; 28:16

Interjecting some passages to support basic facts doesn't make what Paul was teaching true. Beware any references for the Septuagint, as the Greek is altered text – check the Hebrew Scriptures and the record from the Dead Sea Scrolls Bible.

Romans 10

¹⁰ ¹Brethren, my heart's desire and prayer to God for Israel is, that they might be saved. ²For I bear them record that they have a zeal of God, but not according to knowledge. ³For they are being ignorant of God's righteousness, and going about to establish their own righteousness, have not submitted themselves unto the righteousness of God. ⁴For Christ is the end of the law for righteousness to everyone that believeth. ⁵For Moses described the righteousness, which is of the law, That the man which doeth those things shall live by them. ⁶But the righteousness, which is of faith speaks on this wise, Say not in thine heart, Who shall ascend into heaven? (That is, to bring Christ down from above:) ⁷Or, who shall descend into the deep? (That is, to bring up Christ again from the dead.) ⁸But what saith it? The word is nigh thee, even in thy mouth, and in thy heart: that is, the word of faith, which we preach; ⁹That if thou shalt confess with thy mouth the Lord Jesus, and shalt believe in thine heart that God hath raised him from the dead, thou shalt be saved. ¹⁰For with the heart man believeth unto righteousness; and with the mouth confession is made unto salvation. ¹¹For the scripture saith, Whosoever believeth on him shall not be ashamed. ¹²For there is no difference between the Jew and the Greek: for the same Lord over all is rich unto all that call upon him. ¹³For whosoever shall call upon the name of the Lord shall be saved.

"5. Moses writes this about the righteousness that is by the law: "The person who does these things will live by them." Verse 5 is an example of alteration of the Greek from what the correct Hebrew translation is. From the Stone Edition, 4-5; "Carry out My laws and safeguard My decrees to follow them; I am Elohim, your God. You shall observe My decrees, and My laws, which man shall carry out and by which he shall live – I AM Elohim." In Paul's "quote", the words of Elohim are altered to say it is not by doing the will of God as given, but by merely calling upon the name of Jesus: "If you declare with your mouth, "Jesus is Lord," and believe in your heart that God raised him from the dead, you will be saved." Study of Matthew shows Jesus was teaching doing the will of God in reality - both towards God, as well as our fellow mankind, and that we judge ourselves first, so others won't have the need to judge us - and all the Judgments are to be based on how Elohim said we are to live.

As for verse 11 to account "belief" to save – note the end of John 3 for some clarity that is in accord to the OT examples: belief saves, but those who don't obey are condemned. This shows that disobedience is equated to disbelief, as the principle taught in "Why do you call me "Lord", and not do as I say?" Go

back to the Sermon on the Mount – those who do what he taught are wise – those who don't will come to sudden destruction. Also note to not keep the Law (10 Decrees Covenant Standards) (Greek "anomia") are those he will say – in spite of what they wholeheartedly believed – "Depart from me, ye workers of iniquity – I never knew you." The important thing to recognize in the Romans passage above is that Paul is directly defying the explicit words of God by completely altering the conclusion of what God had to say. Elohim declared that by observing and doing His word there is life, we choose to live, that we live through doing them. Paul cuts the verse short in his quote and then inserts his own imagination as the conclusion: [d] that is, the message concerning faith that we proclaim:" and defying what God said about living uprightly by His Standards in the Decree/Covenant. <u>Paul negates everything God said to do, Paul negates everything Jesus said to do, and you have to believe Paul is greater than God, the Prophets and Jesus if you are going to ignore everyone else in the entire Bible to think Paul told the truth. By putting Paul's lies as "Scripture" - all the Bible Publishers and "Theologians" have given false testimony in the name of Elohim Almighty - just because some ancient Council of men said to.</u>

Did God make distinction between Jew and Gentile in the Ten Decrees, Blessings, and Curses? – as the One Law was given for all – by Elohim. He also gave distinction regarding the Land and service at the Temple, also between Jew and Gentile for food laws and certain things about the "appointed times" feasts and such. If God gave instruction – we need to know where we stand. Can't anyone get a genetic test kit to know if they are Jewish – or not? There is no need to pretend or imagine – go with knowable fact and stop pretending what Paul said had any accord to God, the Prophets, Psalms, Writings, or Jesus.

[14] How, then, can they call on the one they have not believed in? And how can they believe in the one of whom they have not heard? And how can they hear without someone preaching to them? [15] And how can anyone preach unless they are sent? As it is written: "How beautiful are the feet of those who bring good news!"

How can anyone know if they should be rejecting the teachings of Paul, unless they are taught the Teachings of God that they know His commandments and know who He commanded that we reject?! Paul is not jumping off the page to tell you he is a liar – you have to observe the Truth to know a lie. It's no wonder God also declared from of old: "My people perish for lack of knowledge;" and its partner passage: "Because you have rejected knowledge, I will also reject you."

[14] How then shall they call on him in whom they have not believed? and how shall they believe in him of whom they have not heard? and how shall they hear without a preacher? [15] And how shall they preach, except they be sent? as it is written, How beautiful are the feet of them

that preach the gospel of peace, and bring glad tidings of good things! [16]But they have not all obeyed the gospel. For Esaias saith, Lord, who hath believed our report? [17]So then faith cometh by hearing, and hearing by the word of God. [18]But I say, Have they not heard? Yes verily, their sound went into all the earth, and their words unto the ends of the world. [19]But I say, Did not Israel know? First Moses saith, I will provoke you to jealousy by them that are no people, and by a foolish nation I will anger you. [20]But Esaias is very bold, and saith, I was found of them that sought me not; I was made manifest unto them that asked not after me. [21]But to Israel he saith, All day long I have stretched forth my hands unto a disobedient and gainsaying people.

Go to the passages referenced and see the message they should have believed. Jesus taught the proper interpretation and application of the Law, Prophets, and Psalms – he taught nothing new. Recall Ezekiel 18 and consider if it is hard to do what is just and right before God and honest men. Which of the Ten Decrees – or any commandment of God – is too hard to understand or do? Which of them causes us to sin? Are you inflamed to dishonor your parents because God said to honor them? Are you inflamed to commit murder, adultery, or theft because God said not to? Are you inflamed to covet everything you see that you don't have – because God said not to covet what others have? Such thoughts are total nonsense. There is no commandment of God or Teaching of Yeshua that is too hard to do or understand – and we not only receive the promised kindness of God for living by them, we should also be a blessing to our family, community, and show how wonderful and simple the Pathway to Life Everlasting is to all who desire to live a just and reasonable life as God wills for all men. We should treat each other with respect and kindness – because we are created in the image of God. We should seek to live in peace with all men – as much as within our ability – but we also see from Abraham that it is just and righteous to rescue the righteous from the wicked. I can think of no other descendant of Abraham to have captured the interest of all the nations as did Yeshua (Jesus). I can think of no other prophet in all Jewish history that should be credited to have done as foretold in Isaiah 42, that he would make keeping the Torah honorable for the Gentiles. I think it's about time we say "Restore!" and "Give it back!", as told in Isaiah 42. Let's get real with God and the Desired One of the ages – "that prophet" Moses foretold of. Preaching faked gospels has done nothing but cause divisions within Christianity and some gospels told make so little sense as to be laughable to those who hear it. It's time to "Restore" the truth of God and Jesus!

Footnotes

ll. Romans 10:5 Lev. 18:5

mm. Romans 10:6 Deut. 30:12

- nn. Romans 10:7 Deut. 30:13
- oo. Romans 10:8 Deut. 30:14
- pp. Romans 10:11 Isaiah 28:16 (see Septuagint)
- qq. Romans 10:13 Joel 2:32
- rr. Romans 10:15 Isaiah 52:7
- ss. Romans 10:16 Isaiah 53:1
- tt. Romans 10:18 Psalm 19:4
- uu. Romans 10:19 Deut. 32:21
- vv. Romans 10:20 Isaiah 65:1
- ww. Romans 10:21 Isaiah 65:2

Romans 11
The Remnant of Israel

¹I ask then: Did God reject his people? By no means! I am an Israelite myself, a descendant of Abraham, from the tribe of Benjamin. ²God did not reject his people, whom he foreknew. Don't you know what Scripture says in the passage about Elijah—how he appealed to God against Israel: ³"Lord, they have killed your prophets and torn down your altars; I am the only one left, and they are trying to kill me"[a]? ⁴And what was God's answer to him? "I have reserved for myself seven thousand who have not bowed the knee to Baal."[b] ⁵ So too, at the present time there is a remnant chosen by grace. ⁶And if by grace, then it cannot be based on works; if it were, grace would no longer be grace.

First, it is now known that Paul was not a Jew, he was a Roman of the Herodian family. Where in Ezekiel did God say the 7000 others had not bowed the knee to Baal because of the grace of God towards the 7000? God was letting Ezekiel know he was not alone – even though he felt at that time he alone stood up for God to the false prophets of Baal and the corrupted king and queen of Israel. Read Ezekiel sometime so you know what went on and that you observe if the grace of God caused the 7000 to remain true to Him – or if the 7000 being true to Him is the reason He will be gracious unto them. Did God say He had kept them BECAUSE they had not bowed their knee to Baal, nor kissed him (Baal) I Kings 19:18? God doesn't go by grace alone – God said to base our decisions on living by His word and doing no evil. Honoring another as God that is not God, but falsehood – that is the source of evil. God warned of the "alien gods" and "gods come lately who are no gods." (Baal and the like) The principle is not hard to grasp, it was in perfect alignment <u>with Ezekiel</u> 18, wherein God is clear to say the soul that sins will be solely responsible for their sins – but the soul who repents to do justice and righteousness in His eyes (by keeping His Decreed Covenant Conditions) will live. The one thing God said He will not absolve anyone of is what? If God is true, this also is important foundational TRUTH – In the Ten Decrees – does God say He will not absolve anyone who falsely testifies in His Name? Go back and read the 3000 year old account and see if this is correct or not. God is just – and it would not be just to punish those who do the will of the Father, and then reward the disobedient with good for being evil or unjust. Paul is artful in his twisting of Scripture and historical fact – but early evidence from the Ebionites says Paul was not a Jew by birth – which would explain his ignorance of the Hebrew Scripture and history – but not his artful

twisting of fact to defy the Instruction and goodness of the Everlasting Covenant and how it relates to the Teachings of Jesus and the judgment of God to be completely just. Did the 7000 not bow their knee to Baal because God did it for them, yet didn't for others? God is not unjust, but rewards each according to their works – not faith alone or grace alone – but by their works. Even Revelation ends on this same note. Paul was not speaking of behalf of God when saying He preserved the 7000 by grace – not that God defies being gracious – but His grace or kindness has purpose and is based on observation of fact. So will we stand with God and believe He is just – or will we stand behind Paul and pretend the Torah is unjust and a weapon formed against us – to lead us to know we cannot do His will and therefore God sacrificed His only Son to serve as a sin sacrifice that He might gain the ungodly by grace alone or faith without works? Was Israel pardoned of their evil by their blood sacrifices? No, as they did not seek to follow the conditions of the Everlasting Covenant ratified at Sinai and had repeatedly rejected Him and His knowledge.**

[7] What then? What the people of Israel sought so earnestly they did not obtain. The elect among them did, but the others were hardened, [8] as it is written:

"God gave them a spirit of stupor, eyes that could not see and ears that could not hear, to this very day."[c]

[9] nd David says: "May their table become a snare and a trap, a stumbling block and a retribution for them. [10] May their eyes be darkened so they cannot see, and their backs be bent forever.

Elect? Where in the Hebrew Scripture or the Teachings of Yeshua do we find that God "elects" one person above another? In the First of the Ten Decrees of God, nothing is said of any "election" of God, but that God is giving instruction via Decrees/Teachings that we prove to God and ourselves and all others – if we are being faithful and true to God by keeping His just standards of righteousness – or not. Nothing about any election of God – just clear – plain – easily observable – perfectly reasonable – perfectly true principles of how God says we are to live. We choose to do what we do – which is why God will hold us accountable for whether we choose life as He gives it – or not. Those who have a spirit of stupor are so because they have not paid attention to believe and observe the true words of God and Jesus. God makes men wise via His word. Those not of God are the fault of stupors – those who reject His instruction are those who are not wise – BECAUSE THEY REJECT HIS INSTRUCTION AND BELIEVE LIES SPOKEN IN HIS NAME. Again – where has God said who He will be gracious to is based on His election? God declared the difference between Jacob and Esau before they did good or evil – but this was His foreknowledge of what they would choose

regarding the promises He had made to Abraham. One would desire His blessing, the other counted it as worth no more than a bowl of food. Why did God say Noah found grace in His eyes? Because of his living justly in the face of injustice, violence and wickedness that prevailed among the evil souls upon the earth? God is not unjust or unreasonable or unfaithful to His word or in giving mankind His word via the descendants of Abraham. Our greatest challenge is to stand up for the unaltered words of God and to reject the altered word and those who altered it or continue to alter it. (Jeremiah 29:23; "Indeed I know, and am a witness, says the LORD." And "we have inherited lies and vanity." Romans shows this is very true.

Ingrafted Branches

[11]Again I ask: Did they stumble so as to fall beyond recovery? Not at all! Rather, because of their transgression, salvation has come to the Gentiles to make Israel envious. [12]But if their transgression means riches for the world, and their loss means riches for the Gentiles, how much greater riches will their full inclusion bring!

Again, I will go over this, God gave instruction before there were Jew and Gentile. In the creation of man, a God given sense of discernment was built into Adam. This is why man is not like any of the other animals of creation, who are indiscriminate about things men are discriminate about by nature. God declared Noah just before the Law was given at Sinai. In fact, God declared Cain was capable to do good and improve himself – after the "fall". Abraham was declared righteous before the Law at Sinai. In fact, Abraham was not found faithful to God based on his genetics – but by his faithfulness to God's leading and instructing him. There are reports that Abraham was schooled with Noah and his sons – see "Jasher." Those of a multitude of nations left Egypt before the giving of the Law – and also ratified the Law at Sinai to be the Covenant – to both Jew and Gentile! Jesus was doing nothing new to renew the Covenant to Jew AND Gentile! The first renewing of the Covenant was done as they entered Canaan. The 160 CE Aramaic English New Testament has Jesus saying <u>he came to renew the Covenant</u> – not give a New Covenant – our records are evidently altered – but God is true, and by going back to see what He declared – we can still know the truth He gave. God did not alter it, and it proves Jesus had to have been directly inspired by God to teach what he did!

[13]I am talking to you Gentiles. Inasmuch as I am the apostle to the Gentiles, I take pride in my ministry [14]in the hope that I may somehow arouse my own people to envy and save some of them.[15]For if their rejection brought reconciliation to the world, what will their

acceptance be but life from the dead? ¹⁶If the part of the dough offered as first fruits is holy, then the whole batch is holy; if the root is holy, so are the branches.

"In as much as I am the apostle to the Gentiles?" In Acts, it is Peter who brought in the first Gentile, but since Acts is suspect at best, we should look to Matthew – wherein Yeshua clearly said to make disciples of all nations – not Jews first, and then Gentiles. The role of Yeshua – the proofs – were not known fully until his death, burial, resurrection, and ascension to the "right hand of the Power on High." There is no mystery regarding Gentiles in Matthew, and it was written before Paul appears on the scene – had Paul bothered to check with the Apostles when he was baptized – if he was baptized. Had he been told to go to someone, that he might know what he must do – I find no reason to think someone as near as Damascus who was a disciple of Yeshua would have not told him of the account of Yeshua by his chosen disciples – how else did Paul come up with pretending to be an "apostle" to the gentiles? How come Paul goes where he can find gentiles who are ignorant of the Hebrew Scripture to foist his "gospel" upon them – pretending to be someone who knew the Scripture – when he obviously was a biblical ignoramus and not even knowing "seed" and "seeds" to be nothing but an invention – as in Hebrew – the language of the Torah – "seed" was always plural – not singular. (so claims Jewish rabbi Tovia Singer) This premise is further known by his alterations of historical fact and citing a Greek translation?!, when someone he claimed to be his teacher would never have supported or used such a faulty "translation". It appears to me that Paul was doing was inventing his "lore" to make biblical ignoramuses of those who would know better if they consulted the Teachings of Yeshua in Matthew and the Hebrew Scripture that the gospel is based upon. Let's see where Paul goes with his invention. In the Torah and Prophets, God spoke of Israel not keeping to His Torah, and as a result they would be cast out of the land of promise and remain few in number – but that a remnant would return to Him. Those who don't believe the doctrines od "Dispensationalism" can show prophecies noted were fulfilled long ago. As God said would happen did happen, and Jews remain few in number to this day – many seek to establish their right to the Land by evil means – and those will end as God declared – as those He will show kindness towards are those who are faithful to do His Covenant conditions faithfully because of His love for them and the goodness, faithfulness and reliability of His word and promises. Read Jeremiah, especially chapters 6 and 16 and it can be observed God was all but fed up with them at that time – and when did it get any better?

¹⁷If some of the branches have been broken off, and you, though a wild olive shoot, have been grafted in among the others and now share in the nourishing sap from the olive root, ¹⁸do not consider yourself to be superior to those other branches. If you do, consider this:

You do not support the root, but the root supports you. ¹⁹You will say then, "Branches were broken off so that I could be grafted in." ²⁰Granted. But they were broken off because of unbelief, and you stand by faith. Do not be arrogant, but tremble. ²¹For if God did not spare the natural branches, he will not spare you either.

The prophets stated the problem with Israel was their rejecting God, which might be seen as "unbelief" so long as one understands the use of "belief" and "unbelief" was directly associated with obedience versus ignoring His Decrees. What nation since unfaithful Judah of Jesus' days has kept the Torah of God to be their manner of life and faith? Jesus said God was tearing the Kingdom from them and would give it to another nation who WOULD produce the fruits of the Kingdom of God. Has Rome been faithful to the Everlasting Covenant? Too much evidence of evil exists to pretend this so. They were the ones who killed thousands, if not millions, forbid the reading of the Holy Scripture by their membership, and foisted the false apostle to be true and supported putting his nonsense into Christian Bibles. God will be true, and we are called to "wait upon the LORD" and trust in His faithfulness to His word. If one trusts in God, one has to take His word as a guide and stay in life – not alter it. However – all the alterations foisted upon us only prove it is time that we non-Jew believers in God acknowledge the passage has now come true that "we have inherited lies and vanity" from those who killed the first generations of faithful believers in Yeshua – both Jew and Gentile. As Yeshua said, all things spoken in the Law and Prophets will be fulfilled – which brings us to Jeremiah 16:19 in the Christian Bible and Jewish Bible (JPS).

King James Version: O Lord, my strength and my fortress, and my refuge in the day of affliction, the Gentiles shall come unto Thee from the ends of the earth and shall say, "Surely our fathers have inherited lies, vanity, and things wherein there is no profit."

New King James: "O Lord, my strength and my fortress, My refuge in the day of affliction, The Gentiles shall come to You From the ends of the earth and say, "Surely our fathers have inherited lies, Worthlessness and unprofitable things."

NIV: "Lord, my strength and my fortress, my refuge in time of distress, to you the nations will come from the ends of the earth and say, "Our ancestors possessed nothing but false gods, worthless idols that did them no good."

JPS: "HASHEM, my Strength, my Stronghold and my Refuge on the day of distress! To You nations will come from the ends of the earth and say: "It was all falsehood that our ancestors inherited, futility that has no purpose. Can a man make gods for himself? – they are not gods!" (This passage appears to be missing in the Dead Sea Scrolls Bible.)

Jesus/Yeshua never claimed to be God – he prayed to God – he said to keep His commandments faithfully – to the least of the commandments! – so long as the heavens and earth shall last – not until he was killed on the cross! The Everlasting Covenant was given to Jew and Gentile at the same time – the gospel message taught by Jesus was also to be given to Jew and Gentile – the Great Commission said to make disciples of all the nations and that they were to be taught what Jesus had first taught them – not one gospel for the Jews and another for the Gentiles, or one gospel for those before the cross, and a different message for those after his resurrection.

22Consider therefore the kindness and sternness of God: sternness to those who fell, but kindness to you, provided that you continue in his kindness. Otherwise, you also will be cut off. 23And if they do not persist in unbelief, they will be grafted in, for God is able to graft them in again. 24After all, if you were cut out of an olive tree that is wild by nature, and contrary to nature were grafted into a cultivated olive tree, how much more readily will these, the natural branches, be grafted into their own olive tree!

Gentiles being included with Israel in the kindness of God is based on the Torah – the very words already spoken by God at Sinai – in fulfillment to His promise to bless all nations through the seed of Abraham. Read your Bible and see this is so. Lies against the Everlasting Covenant are a great evil – whether foisted by fake Christians or fake Jews.

All Israel Will Be Saved

25I do not want you to be ignorant of this mystery, brothers and sisters, so that you may not be conceited: Israel has experienced a hardening in part until the full number of the Gentiles has come in, 26and in this way[e] all Israel will be saved. As it is written:

"The deliverer will come from Zion; he will turn godlessness away from Jacob. 27And this is[f] my covenant with them when I take away their sins."[g]

28As far as the gospel is concerned, they are enemies for your sake; but as far as election is concerned, they are loved on account of the patriarchs, 29for God's gifts and his call are irrevocable. 30Just as you who were at one time disobedient to God have now received mercy as a result of their disobedience, 31so they too have now become disobedient in order that they too may now[h] receive mercy as a result of God's mercy to you. 32For God has bound everyone over to disobedience so that he may have mercy on them all.

God has bound no one to disobedience – rather God has said that He desires all men to repent that He might save them! Go to the Holy Scripture and pay attention to the words of God – very close attention – stop trusting in those who testify against the Law and the Testimony. God gave His Instructions in righteousness to elevate and bless us – if we will observe His Instruction to do them! The main

passage sited in the footnotes is from Isaiah 59: 20-21. God did not "harden" Israel in Isaiah 59. In fact, God was pleading for them to return to Him by doing as He instructed – they had no fear of God and were bent on following their own ways – not the God given pathway to life! Read all of Isaiah 59 and see it was not God who hardened Israel's heart – so Paul once again testifies against the Law and the Prophets. Why have we and our "fathers" been so blinded all these years? It's time to return to God and believe His word, Covenant and will for men of all nations.

"But the righteousness that is by faith says: "Do not say in your heart, 'Who will ascend into heaven?'" [b](that is, to bring Christ down) 7"or 'Who will descend into the deep?'" [c](that is, to bring Christ up from the dead). 8But what does it say? "The word is near you; it is in your mouth and in your heart," [d]that is, the message concerning faith that we proclaim: 9If you declare with your mouth, "Jesus is Lord," and believe in your heart that God raised him from the dead, you will be saved."

Look back at the dialogue of Exodus 20 and Deuteronomy 4. Elohim said the Standards of the Covenant are near to us, in our hearts and mouth - they are perfectly reasonable - they are universal standards - anyone should realize each of them is based on the differences between what is good and what is evil to any reasonable and normal human being. He also said we are capable and responsible to both Him and our fellow. No where is it possible or implied that anything was a mystery that one might ask who will ascend to the heavens to get it to tell us, or who will cross the seas to find it for us? No, God said it is near to us and in our hearts and mouths!, not some "Mystery" of any kind. Think this over. Look at the Covenant Standards from the days of Ezekiel, although not as deeply rooted to the teachings of Jesus - look over the current account in all our "Bibles" - the fact is that Paul was retelling his delusions - Paul was not faithful to tell us what God or Jesus taught!!!! In fact - Paul was defying God, Moses, every person present at Sinai, all the Prophets, as well as the very one he claimed to have appointed him to tell his lies to the non-Jew Gentiles!!!! If you cannot see that flagrant lie - you'd just as well stop reading the Bible and join Judaism, Islam, Mormonism, or the Church of Satan - because you do not believe God or His holy prophets!!!.

<u>**Jesus never taught that his keeping the Torah would be substituted for us not keeping the Torah.**</u> **No, instead he taught repenting and going back and keeping the Covenant as God gave it – not as the unfaithful of his days commanded that was not in accord to the Covenant decrees God. According to Jesus, faith is one of the weightier matters of the Law, and per the example of Abraham and all those counted as faithful to God – their faithfulness was accounted to them. As Yeshua taught about the resurrection – we trust not only in the blessing and kindness in our current life – but also in the rewards to come when God judges the just and the**

unjust – the righteous and the wicked. Reward is based on our works – to have done the works of God, as instructed by God – or to have refused to walk in the pathways of life as He instructed.

If our love for Elohim or Jesus (Joshua) is true - we need to absolutely reject Paul's lies and stand up for the real truth of God. Use the Teachings of God to know who is true to God, from who is not. Then you will be able to distinguish between truth versus lies, or good versus evil, or who actually serves Elohim from him who does not. This is exactly what Elohim declared as necessary for today, as we are in an age of great deceit.

Doxology

[33]Oh, the depth of the riches of the wisdom and [i]knowledge of God! How unsearchable his judgments, and his paths beyond tracing out!

God gave Instruction via Moses and at Sinai directly – His word is not hard to understand or to keep and He invites us to know and do His will that He might bless us. Read Psalm 119 if one seeks to regard His good will. The Law is wisdom and knowledge given by God Himself and are not beyond discovery or understanding! God said so. Do you disbelieve God because Paul said His word is too hard to understand or do? What seems "impossible" in the Sermon on the Mount is viewed "impossible" because the words of Yeshua were altered. See the Hebrew Gospel of Matthew and carefully note the alteration and the impart it has towards understanding the truth Yeshua spoke. Yeshua didn't alter the words of God – the words of Yeshua were altered. This alone proves John questionable as it testifies that "my words shall by no means pass away", as they were altered.

[34]"Who has known the mind of the Lord? Or who has been his counselor?"

How can we know the mind of God if we don't first hear what He had to say, and then judge if Paul spoke on His behalf or not? How can we "know" the gospel of God taught by Yeshua unless we first grasp his teachings in Matthew as they also find accord to the words of God in the Torah and prophets? How can we judge justly unless we see if Yeshua spoke the truth in Matthew? Matthew is the best record of his teachings and is reported to have been written by his apostles in Hebrew very early in Church history. What God has given us to know is what we need – but we cannot say YHVH is our God and then spurn and reject His instruction and commandment (Torah) – as those who reject doing His will are His enemies – not those He will bless. (so says the first of the Ten Decrees)

[35]"Who has ever given to God, that God should repay them?"[k] [36]For from him and through him and for him are all things. To him be the glory forever! Amen.

If God says He will bless and show His kindness towards those whose love for Him is true to His Covenant – it is His goodness and blessing to give those who "earn" it by love and faithfulness and trust in Him and His instructions. His instruction was given that we not be foolish – but become wise through knowing His instruction and the pathway for which mankind, according to mankind's God given nature, was created to live justly, love mercy and walk humbly with Him. His blessing and kindness are His just reward! Where does God ever say He will reward the wicked the same as He will those who are righteous in His sight? In one hand the discovery of the God given pathway to life and freedom to live life at its fullest – on the other is a life than leads to death and multitudes of problems – which God was true to tell: "Choose life, that ye may live!" The letters of the Law no more bring death and a curse, than the flesh of a person cause sin – the soul chooses life or death by whether it chooses to trust in God and His faithfulness to His word - or if the soul does not trust the pathway of justice, fairness, mercy and truth given by God. God is being true to His word to give just recompense to what a person chooses to do. Paul is creating a "straw-man" argument and evidently has no knowledge of the Torah or God or His word or promises and Covenants.

By all means – check out the passages in the footnotes – but do so with eyes open to seek to understand the will of God – especially in context to claims from Paul – see if Paul is taking Jewish scripture in proper context – or if the passage is not being taken in context. Sometimes study Bibles and Paul use scripture in a "cute and paste" manner that shows lack of understanding. Most are hit and miss. Sometimes they prove mistranslations exist in Christian Bibles. These kinds of things are what made discovery of the truth difficult – not God.

Don't forget who Yeshua claimed to be in Matthew. The proof between a true prophet and a false prophet is what they tell you to believe or do – is it in accord with the words of God to Adam and Eve, Cain, Noah, Abraham, Isaac, Jacob, Moses – the prophets – and finally the teachings of Yeshua in the Hebrew Gospel of Matthew – or is it only true to the Greek to English translation of Matthew? Come to know the truth, as it will set you free indeed as you are a disciple indeed.

Footnotes

a. Romans 11:3 1 Kings 19:10,14
b. Romans 11:4 1 Kings 19:18
c. Romans 11:8 Deut. 29:4; Isaiah 29:10
d. Romans 11:10 Psalm 69:22,23
e. Romans 11:26 Or *and so*
f. Romans 11:27 Or *will be*

g. Romans 11:27 Isaiah 59:20,21; 27:9 (see Septuagint); Jer. 31:33,34
h. Romans 11:31 Some manuscripts do not have *now*.
i. Romans 11:33 Or *riches and the wisdom and the*
j. Romans 11:34 Isaiah 40:13
k. Romans 11:35 Job 41:11

Romans 12
A Living Sacrifice

¹Therefore, I urge you, brothers, and sisters, in view of God's mercy, to offer your bodies as a living sacrifice, holy and pleasing to God—this is your true and proper worship. ²Do not conform to the pattern of this world but be transformed by the renewing of your mind. Then you will be able to test and approve what God's will is—his good, pleasing, and perfect will.

Where in the Everlasting Covenant did God say He demands man to offer their bodies as a living sacrifice? No where that I've found. Is this what God meant when saying: "What does God require of thee, O man, but to live justly, love mercy and walk humbly with thy God"? Is this what the wise man who said: "Fear God and keep His commandments – this is the duty of man."? God declared "My Covenant" to be the Ten Decrees – not "613 Laws" that are impossible for any man to keep. God did warn not to be conformed to the world of those who serve other gods – gods of their own creation, or the "alien gods" who "are no gods" and "gods come lately." God revealed Himself to Jew and Gentile at Sinai – and we would do well and review His words that we might be amongst those who are blessed by knowing His revealing of Himself at the same time that He gave just and righteous commandments that are completely true and that were given to elevate all who would repent and turn to observe and do His will and Covenant.

If God gave His word to bless and elevate us – to cause us to grow in doing what is just and right in His sight – then we absolutely must align our conscience to the words of God – that we might be walking humbly with our God in accepting His pathways and walking within His stated pathway of life. If we cast aside His pathway to then walk on a pathway that He warned against – we have not trusted God, just as Adam and Eve didn't trust God in the Garden by partaking of the tree of the knowledge of good and evil but chose to believe a lie of the Serpent. Trials are given along our lives so that both God and ourselves can know whether we will obey Him – or not. I'll choose this day to follow God – even though and old song says: "It was good for Paul and Silas, it's good enough for me." No, rather: It was good for Moses and Jesus – that's good enough for me! I'll choose to live life that is true to God and that gives me full freedom to do justly and rightly – to live life in equality with other men, and a life that gives God given rights – not servitude or communism. See the Ten Decrees: they don't support servitude, Communism, or Socialism – the words of God tell us what the best pathway to live within! It's a

mystery to me how both Communism and Psychology were both birthed by Jews…. God gave no such instruction to them. And what was the message of Jesus to the Jews, since he knew the kingdom was being torn from them and the Temple would be destroyed and the remnant scattered throughout the world?

Humble Service in the Body of Christ

[3]For by the grace given me I say to every one of you: Do not think of yourself more highly than you ought, but rather think of yourself with sober judgment, in accordance with the faith God has distributed to each of you. [4]For just as each of us has one body with many members, and these members do not all have the same function, [5]so in Christ we, though many, form one body, and each member belongs to all the others. [6]We have different gifts, according to the grace given to each of us. If your gift is prophesying, then prophesy in accordance with your[a] faith; [7]if it is serving, then serve; if it is teaching, then teach; [8]if it is to encourage, then give encouragement; if it is giving, then give generously; if it is to lead ,[b]do it diligently; if it is to show mercy, do it cheerfully.

Where is Paul's telling of the God given pathways established throughout the Hebrew Scripture? Judgment should be based on judging as God decreed – not according to some imaginary "faith" that God distributed among the disciples of Paul – those who put the words of Paul above the words of God and Yeshua. I don't belong to you, and you don't belong to me – each of us belong to God – but who choses His pathways to live by? Where did Yeshua teach God would give us differing "gifts"? Where did God say he would give us each different "gifts"? I've heard many who claim the gift of prophecy that made no sense at all. I've seen many who pretend the "gift" of speaking in tongues – but no such thing is found in the mouth of Yeshua in Matthew – only in Mark – a reported disciple of Paul. I've seen many who claim the "gift" of miraculous healing – but have also seen corruption and guile amongst them enough to know that what they did was not of God – because God let us know how to tell who speaks on His behalf, just as we were also informed how to tell those who DO NOT – miracles alone were not proof. God does not want His people to be ignorant of His will, as He said "My people perish for lack of knowledge." Surely the knowing of His will. Paul claimed to have great knowledge – but was an abject ignoramus of God's will. Did he teach others to value him more than he deserved? It sure appears so to me.

Love in Action

The following is perhaps the closest Paul gets to the truth of God. Much of this can be referred to from the teachings of Yeshua in Matthew – although footnotes give no credit to showing principles from the Law being in the teachings of Jesus in Matthew. Where Paul goes off track is that God created men to live in equality –

not that men were told to put everyone else above themselves – God and Yeshua taught equality among men, as men are created in the image of God – and that He alone is God – and we are all brethren who abide in His will and care. The Ten Decrees are based on this principle – not the principle of servitude to anyone but God and "him to which it is due." In the Torah, the unity between men of all nations (Jew and Gentile) was found in all having the same law to live by – the gracious instructions in righteousness – as given by God.

[9] Love must be sincere. Hate what is evil; cling to what is good. [10] Be devoted to one another in love. Honor one another above yourselves. [11] Never be lacking in zeal, but keep your spiritual fervor, serving the Lord. [12] Be joyful in hope, patient in affliction, faithful in prayer. [13] Share with the Lord's people who are in need. Practice hospitality.

[14] Bless those who persecute you; bless and do not curse. [15] Rejoice with those who rejoice; mourn with those who mourn. [16] Live in harmony with one another. Do not be proud, but be willing to associate with people of low position.[c] Do not be conceited.

[17] Do not repay anyone evil for evil. Be careful to do what is right in the eyes of everyone. [18] If it is possible, as far as it depends on you, live at peace with everyone. [19] Do not take revenge, my dear friends, but leave room for God's wrath, for it is written: "It is mine to avenge; I will repay."[d] says the Lord. [20] On the contrary:

"If your enemy is hungry, feed him; if he is thirsty, give him something to drink. In doing this, you will heap burning coals on his head."[e] [21] Do not be overcome by evil, but overcome evil with good.

Footnotes

l. Romans 12:6 Or *the*

m. Romans 12:8 Or *to provide for others*

n. Romans 12:16 Or *willing to do menial work*

o. Romans 12:19 Deut. 32:35

p. Romans 12:20 Prov. 25:21,22

Romans 13
Submission to Governing Authorities

¹Let everyone be subject to the governing authorities, for there is no authority except that which God has established. The authorities that exist have been established by God. ²Consequently, whoever rebels against the authority is rebelling against what God has instituted, and those who do so will bring judgment on themselves. ³For rulers hold no terror for those who do right, but for those who do wrong. Do you want to be free from fear of the one in authority? Then do what is right and you will be commended. ⁴For the one in authority is God's servant for your good. But if you do wrong, be afraid, for rulers do not bear the sword for no reason. They are God's servants, agents of wrath to bring punishment on the wrongdoer. ⁵Therefore, it is necessary to submit to the authorities, not only because of possible punishment but also as a matter of conscience.

⁶This is also why you pay taxes, for the authorities are God's servants, who give their full time to governing. ⁷Give to everyone what you owe them: If you owe taxes, pay taxes; if revenue, then revenue; if respect, then respect; if honor, then honor.

Where did God say this about Roman rulers – as these are who ruled over the land in Paul's days – and God allows trials to see if we will obey Him – or not. What was the instruction of God to Israel after the remnant returned from Babylon? What was Yeshua's instruction to Israel when he arrived on the scene? Were they being faithful to God as He had instructed them? No. A group of the faithful had long since separated themselves from Jerusalem with cause and gone to Quamran, and evidently John the Baptist was from this group. Jews have long held the view that Rome is their perpetual enemy – and Roman influence continues to this day – in government and in Scripture for Christians – books the Roman Church decreed to be in the Christian Bible, and Rome also went along with alterations to the Hebrew Scripture in the Christian Scripture – for the benefit of our belief in Paul – particularly as found here in Romans 13. In Matthew we see Jesus showing that it is possible to be a Christian in a Roman ruled world. The Roman rulers sought to free him – it was the Jewish leadership that desired his death. Jesus taught paying taxes and living justly – and no government that rules justly would demand otherwise. What we should all see is that by our time many governments have been corrupted to do evil and lie to their people directly and via control of the propaganda spewed by the licensed News Media – lies prevail – not truth. Accusations are pretended to sway public "opinion polls" to lull our minds from obvious facts – if they were ever reported on. God is who we owe allegiance to –

not government. Did Danial obey God when he prayed towards Jerusalem? Did Peter obey God when saying he must obey God, rather than man? God gave instruction to know who He said to obey. As Jesus pointed out about taxes: "Whose image is on the coin?" and that we are to give to God what is rightfully His, and to man, that which is of man and due a man. No man is God – in spite of what Roman rulers or the Pope call themselves. If you think the USA is of God to be obeyed without question – read "Apollyon Rising – 2012", or watch "Brotherhood of Darkness" on YouTube by Stanley Montif. Rome put Paul in our Bibles to get us to obey them – not to cause us to serve God according to His word. Have not governments sought to stamp out belief in God and His pathway to live life? If you don't see this – you've blinded yourself by believing Paul or disbelieving God.

Love Fulfills the Law

[8]Let no debt remain outstanding, except the continuing debt to love one another, for whoever loves others has fulfilled the law. [9]The commandments, "You shall not commit adultery," "You shall not murder," "You shall not steal," "You shall not covet," [a]and whatever other command there may be, are summed up in this one command: "Love your neighbor as yourself." [b] [10]Love does no harm to a neighbor. Therefore, love is the fulfillment of the law.

Here is another bait and switch job by Paul. Go back to Matthew and focus on what Yeshua taught. Yeshua taught that love is a principle that proper understanding of the Law requires – love – the Law hangs on the peg of love as a secure foundation. First that love for God observes His word to do it – second – that doing the Law is to be done with love towards God – to then be reflected in our love towards others in keeping the more obvious commandments of how we live towards each other. The love of God has observable definition – identifiable by what it does – not some imagined standard that flows outside the boundaries given by God. Is love a debt? Or is it the response of what should come naturally to someone who lives by the word of God? Does love excuse us from the Law – or is love in full accord with the Law and Covenant ratified at Sinai?

The Day Is Near

[11]And do this, understanding the present time: The hour has already come for you to wake up from your slumber, because our salvation is nearer now than when we first believed. [12]The night is nearly over; the day is almost here. So let us put aside the deeds of darkness and put on the armor of light. [13]Let us behave decently, as in the daytime, not in carousing and drunkenness, not in sexual immorality and debauchery, not in dissension

and jealousy. ¹⁴Rather, clothe yourselves with the Lord Jesus Christ, and do not think about how to gratify the desires of the flesh.

Once again, Paul pits flesh against the soul, as though the flesh is the cause of sin, not the heart that is outside the pathway of life given by God. Paul is presenting extremes, so there isn't objection to say those extreme behaviors are some kind of enlightenment that can only be discerned by the "spirit" or spiritual armor. However – since we should all be able to see the lies Paul foisted in the NAME of God and Yeshua – the time has come to awaken from our spiritual slumber to have not noticed following Paul requires disrespect and disregard for the words of God in the Torah. True life is known when one is walking in the God given pathways of life – not the imaginations of Paul – who didn't tell the truth on the words of God – but sowed discord instead.

Footnotes

q. Romans 13:9 Exodus 20:13-15,17; Deut. 5:17-19,21

r. Romans 13:9 Lev. 19:18

s. Romans 13:14 In contexts like this, the Greek word for *flesh (sarx)* refers to the sinful state of human beings, often presented as a power in opposition to the Spirit.

Romans 14
The Weak and the Strong

¹Accept the one whose faith is weak, without quarreling over disputable matters. ²One person's faith allows them to eat anything, but another, whose faith is weak, eats only vegetables. ³The one who eats everything must not treat with contempt the one who does not, and the one who does not eat everything must not judge the one who does, for God has accepted them. ⁴Who are you to judge someone else's servant? To their own master, servants stand or fall. And they will stand, for the Lord is able to make them stand.

On the surface this seems reasonable – not to quarrel over disputable matters. However, are the matters Paul defines as disputable that the Instructions of God in the Everlasting Covenant deem prohibited? Indeed, the perceptions given by Paul disregard the distinctions God gave! Every word of God was given for a purpose – don't set them aside because Paul said so! What has faith to do with what we eat, except if God had commanded or prohibited something, or had prohibited it for one group (children of Abraham), and not for another (those of the multitude of nations). For example – there is prohibition against eating blood – for both Jew and Gentile. Since God prohibited this because the life is contained in the blood – all who seek to do His will must not do that which He prohibited – because He said so, and because the oldest records in the Dead Sea Scrolls also affirm this is not an addition or alteration. And what of being a vegetarian? What has God said? When Daniel refused the kings food it was likely with cause that he had no assurance it was in keeping with the food laws for the children of Israel. Daniel likely chose to eat vegetarian so he could know he was not eating anything God prohibited him to eat. Daniel was very beloved by God. God never said Daniel was "weak in the faith." Another example is Peter – who is said to have been a vegetarian. I can't help but think of the words of Paul against Peter in Galatians. Peter likely chose to eat vegetarian to ensure he was not eating prohibited things when visiting gentiles taught by Paul – or Jews taught by Paul, if the Jews dared believe him. One prohibited thing were sacrifices to Idols (demons). Some have said it was common to get meat from a market that may have had such meat. I honestly wonder about this myself because if Noah was told it was fine to eat of any animal – why would God then tell Israel there were detestable things? Seems wildly inconsistent to me. Some may have practiced child sacrifice and eating them, and I most suspect this was the original condition, as it was told about those who were in the Land before them who had become very wicked. I've heard

reports of this today in RSA cults, and some in the dark recesses of weird branches in Judaism, and was documented in the 1400's. That should be known as a high possibility given the vast alterations done to Deuteronomy that can be seen between the five pages of "V" versus the 34 chapters of Deuteronomy. Note in Acts that Peter's conclusion about a vision of detestable food had to do with taking the gospel to the gentiles – not God altering His food laws for the children of Israel. If you want to know if you are Jewish or not, so you might be faithful to every word that proceeds from the mouth of God – by all means – get a genetic test and see fact – not some imagination from Paul that would have God defying His own Covenant and word. It may be true that it is as Jesus taught – it is not that which goes into a person that defiles them, it is what they think and do. For myself, I don't fret over food because the Oldest Covenant account (V) has not food prohibitions, and the clarity of the words of God in Isaiah 56 don't say anything about it, but per Jeremiah, we need to seek "the old paths" – and one cannot get any older than 'V' at this time. It makes perfect sense to me.

If we serve and obey the one true God – it is to Him we stand or fall. God does not make His enemies (those who reject His word) to stand. As Yeshua taught in Matthew, there would be a day that many would call him "Lord!", and he would tell them; "Depart from me, ye workers of iniquity (Torahless), I never knew you." (Torah meaning the Teachings of God, not the writings of the rabbinical oral torahs.)

It's also needful to know the Instructions of God to Israel in the dispersion amongst the nations of the world, which is a study I'm reviewing now from the writings of "Jews Against Zionism" from Monsey, NY. They have much to say against the Jewish Zionists to be a very evil influence that has no part in the Torah of God. How much have Jews been lead away by Zionists from the paths God declared they were to live in the diaspora? As Yeshua said: all has to be fulfilled. How can believers in God, the one true God, who seek to worship Him alone, find accord to support faithful Jews in spite of the Zionists? Surely we should give ear to their cries and pleadings and warnings.

[5]One person considers one day more sacred than another; another considers every day alike. Each of them should be fully convinced in their own mind. [6]Whoever regards one day as special does so to the Lord. Whoever eats meat does so to the Lord, for they give thanks to God; and whoever abstains does so to the Lord and gives thanks to God. [7]For none of us lives for ourselves alone, and none of us dies for ourselves alone. [8]If we live, we live for the Lord; and if we die, we die for the Lord. So, whether we live or die, we belong to the Lord. [9]For this very reason, Christ died and returned to life so that he might be the Lord of both the dead and the living.

Did God, at Creation, distinguish and set aside the Seventh Day as holy? In the Ten Decrees given by God as Sinai, did God restate the importance to keep the Seventh Day holy and distinguished from the secular six days that preceded it? Did He say that we are to accomplish our work in six days, but the Seventh Day is Holy and a day of rest from labor/work? If God gave this decree to all present at Sinai – Jew and Gentile – keeping the Sabbath holy is for all who claim to believe God. The Sabbath was given as an everlasting ordinance – not temporary until the cross. Yeshua taught keeping the Sabbath. The distinction given in his teachings is to know it is lawful to do good on the Sabbath – through preserving life and through healing or rescuing from danger. Few Churches will consider the Sabbath, but it really doesn't matter as an individual or family, as the weekly Sabbath was kept in the home.

God also gave appointed times in various special days that have distinction between Jew and non-Jew. For example, God gave the Passover, but a non-Jew was not to partake of it with a Jewish family unless they had been circumcised. Another would be the feast of Tabernacles – Jew and Gentile were to keep it, as it was a reminder of God leading them both out of Egypt to freedom to worship Him alone the One True God. These matters are needful to look into further, once our hearts and minds are freed from the lies taught by Paul. If God declared differently than Paul – be advised – God is allowing us to be tested – to see if we will obey Him – or not! As for me – I'm through with Paul. I'm putting this information out there so you don't have to be ignorant as I was – this information is for those searching for and seeking TRUTH given by God and Yeshua. Also review Matthew (HGOM) and see why Yeshua rose from the dead. God is the God of the living and the dead, and Yeshua never claimed to be divine or God or a literal half-God, half man. As "son of man" he was mortal – God raised him up and he reportedly ascended to the right hand of the Power on High as prophesied in Daniel.

[10] You, then, why do you judge your brother or sister [a]? Or why do you treat them with contempt? For we will all stand before God's judgment seat. [11] It is written:

"'As surely as I live,' says the Lord, 'every knee will bow before me; every tongue will acknowledge God.'"[b]

[12] So then, each of us will give an account of ourselves to God.

[13] Therefore let us stop passing judgment on one another. Instead, make up your mind not to put any stumbling block or obstacle in the way of a brother or sister. [14] I am convinced, being fully persuaded in the Lord Jesus, that nothing is unclean in itself. But if anyone regards something as unclean, then for that person it is unclean. [15] If your brother or sister is distressed because of what you eat, you are no longer acting in love. Do not by your eating destroy someone for whom Christ died. [16] Therefore do not let what you know is good be

spoken of as evil. ¹⁷For the kingdom of God is not a matter of eating and drinking, but of righteousness, peace and joy in the Holy Spirit, ¹⁸because anyone who serves Christ in this way is pleasing to God and receives human approval.

No man has the authority or right to set aside any word of God – not Moses, Jesus, or Paul. Don't let what God said is good be called evil. Don't let the judgment God commanded be used to be set aside for anyone claiming to speak on behalf of God. See if they tell the truth – See if they tell you to set aside what God said those who love Him will do – see if they speak according to the Law and the Testimony – or not. If you choose to disbelieve God – don't blame God for your disbelief and disobedience. The kingdom of God is about those who believe and obey God. Those who follow their own hearts have not humbled themselves before God. The "Spirit" will not testify against the words of God – so beware thinking you are following God by doing as Paul says – you are likely just going to be as ignorant as he was and be following your own imaginations/interpretations of Paul and thinking it is God speaking to you.

¹⁹Let us therefore make every effort to do what leads to peace and to mutual edification. ²⁰Do not destroy the work of God for the sake of food. All food is clean, but it is wrong for a person to eat anything that causes someone else to stumble. ²¹It is better not to eat meat or drink wine or to do anything else that will cause your brother or sister to fall.

It's far better to know the one true God and what His will and blessings are. Did the true prophets cower in the face of the false prophets? Do true prophets believe false prophets? One does not need to be a prophet or "spiritual" to see Paul was a total ignoramus who led people away from God given truth – to believe his mythology.

²²So whatever you believe about these things keep between yourself and God. Blessed is the one who does not condemn himself by what he approves. ²³But whoever has doubts is condemned if they eat, because their eating is not from faith; and everything that does not come from faith is sin.

God defined sin – not Paul. Yeshua affirmed that his disciples will live by every word of God – and being humble before God is to accept His judgments to be completely true and reliable. What God said is sin is sin. What God said is just and right. It is not about what we believe, unless we believe what God said. Rather than pretend it is about human individual opinions – it's time to re-investigate what God said sin is and stop pretending that what we think is more valid than the word and decree of God.

The passage from Isaiah 45:23 is true, but Paul is not using it uprightly. Since every knee will bow – it's better to repent and believe God now than after it is too late. "Choose life that you may live."

Footnotes

t. Romans 14:10 The Greek word for *brother or sister (adelphos)* refers here to a believer, whether man or woman, as part of God's family; also in verses 13, 15 and 21.

u. Romans 14:11 Isaiah 45:23

v. Romans 14:23 Some manuscripts place 16:25-27 here; others after 15:33.

Romans 15

After many years of studying Pauline letters, particularly Romans, as understood by Protestant and Reformation viewpoints – one thing that helped me understand Paul better was to take what he said one thing at a time and see if it contains common sense advice and then to double check his material quotes to the Scripture – in particular the Teachings given by Jesus, which led me to the words of God in the Torah, Prophets and Psalms – these were well understood by Jesus and represented very well in his teachings. Since we are reaching the end of Romans – it might prove helpful to examine each statement by Paul individually so we don't mentally draw a blanket over his claims and pretend we understand what he said – we can see if he is making good clear sense - or not. Mainly to see if he was teaching according to the word of God or not.

¹We who are strong ought to bear with the failings of the weak and not to please ourselves.

Paul's definition of who is weak and who is strong is often backwards to the Instructions given by God, and often is devoid of acknowledging His stated standard – the Law and Torah. We should help the weak, but not just enabling them. Any reasonable person can see we are all at different levels of maturity, and the younger might well be advised to consider you may not yet understand as much as someone else with more experience – learn to help each other – don't just "bear with the failings of the weak."

²Each of us should please our neighbors for their good, to build them up.

Then why did Paul put down the apostles of Jesus and Jewish Christians who followed the pathway to life as taught by Yeshua? Dare we call out hypocrite?

³For even Christ did not please himself but, as it is written: "The insults of those who insult you have fallen on me."[a] ⁴For everything that was written in the past was written to teach us, so that through the endurance taught in the Scriptures and the encouragement they provide we might have hope.

Now Paul flips on his head to tell the truth. God gave the Torah to bless and enlighten all who seek to do His will – to elevate us towards Him – to become all we can be – to be transformed from ignorance to wisdom. We learn from God, as He is our Teacher when we live by His word and search out His Law as did David – which is well spoken in Psalm 119. If God said we are capable and responsible to do better and overcome sin, that it not overcome us – why put down the Law as some impossible feat to know and do – when God said it was not too hard to

understand or do? True hope resides in God being faithful to His Torah and Covenant, and we learn faithfulness by observing the Covenant to do it.

⁵May the God who gives endurance and encouragement give you the same attitude of mind toward each other that Christ Jesus had, ⁶so that with one mind and one voice you may glorify the God and Father of our Lord Jesus Christ.

Since we know Paul did not meet Jesus – there is no way he understood or knew the "attitude of mind" that Jesus had. God spoke clearly when giving the conditions to the Everlasting Covenant. There are those He will bless, and there are those He holds in judgment – even though judgment is delayed – time and trials in life are what prove our faithfulness to Him. This is told throughout history in the Bible. This is also spoken of in Jesus' parables about the Kingdom of God and who were faithful and wise servants. Both agree that God does not give an attitude and endurance modeled after Jesus – it is our responsibility to develop throughout our lives. If God is the one giving endurance – are those who accept His instruction readily, but fade out and die because they have little or no root within themselves to sustain doing rightly and justly – is God to blame for their NOT continuing in faithfulness? If it is a gift of God – how can He be just to judge the unenduring who turn from righteousness to do evil? God forbid any man judge God for what the man was responsible to do! God can give us good instructions, but we have to participate in doing His will! This is the main problem with the mistranslations of "seed" versus "seeds" – from the beginning God said it is our responsibility to do justly – to live according to His word. Those who disregard His instruction as needful are in for a world of hurt when they realize Paul told a story on God that just isn't so – and as Yeshua said, those who are anti-Law of God are those he will tell: "Depart from me, I never knew you." Jesus said to honor God by doing His will. One either follows the instructions of God and those found true to His instruction – or one does not. The Law brings life and order. Following the Teachings given by Jesus' result in living life to be reasonable, just, merciful and blessed of God. Pretending God has grace towards His enemies is denial of the Covenant and every warning or promise God gave. There is no accord with truth and lies – and pretending there is has been the source of great evils for centuries.

⁷Accept one another, then, just as Christ accepted you, in order to bring praise to God. ⁸For I tell you that Christ has become a servant of the Jews[b] on behalf of God's truth, so that the promises made to the patriarchs might be confirmed ⁹and, moreover, that the Gentiles might glorify God for his mercy. As it is written:

"Therefore I will praise you among the Gentiles; I will sing the praises of your name."[c] 10

Again, it says, "Rejoice, you Gentiles, with his people."[d]

¹¹ And again, "Praise the Lord, all you Gentiles; let all the peoples extol him."[e]

¹² And again, Isaiah says,"The Root of Jesse will spring up, one who will arise to rule over the nations; in him the Gentiles will hope."[f]

¹³ May the God of hope fill you with all joy and peace as you trust in him, so that you may overflow with hope by the power of the Holy Spirit.

Paul the Minister to the Gentiles

¹⁴I am convinced, my brothers and sisters, that you yourselves are full of goodness, filled with knowledge and competence to instruct one another.¹⁵Yet I have written you quite boldly on some points to remind you of them again, because of the grace God gave me ¹⁶to be a minister of Christ Jesus to the Gentiles. He gave me the priestly duty of proclaiming the gospel of God, so that the Gentiles might become an offering acceptable to God, sanctified by the Holy Spirit.

¹⁷Therefore I glory in Christ Jesus in my service to God. ¹⁸I will not venture to speak of anything except what Christ has accomplished through me in leading the Gentiles to obey God by what I have said and done— ¹⁹by the power of signs and wonders, through the power of the Spirit of God. So from Jerusalem all the way around to Illyricum, I have fully proclaimed the gospel of Christ. ²⁰It has always been my ambition to preach the gospel where Christ was not known, so that I would not be building on someone else's foundation. ²¹Rather, as it is written:

"Those who were not told about him will see, and those who have not heard will understand."[g]

²²This is why I have often been hindered from coming to you.

Paul's Plan to Visit Rome

²³But now that there is no more place for me to work in these regions, and since I have been longing for many years to visit you, ²⁴I plan to do so when I go to Spain. I hope to see you while passing through and to have you assist me on my journey there, after I have enjoyed your company for a while. ²⁵Now, however, I am on my way to Jerusalem in the service of the Lord's people there. ²⁶For Macedonia and Achaia were pleased to make a contribution for the poor among the Lord's people in Jerusalem. ²⁷They were pleased to do it, and indeed they owe it to them. For if the Gentiles have shared in the Jews' spiritual blessings, they owe it to the Jews to share with them their material blessings. ²⁸So after I have completed this task and have made sure that they have received this contribution, I will go to Spain and visit you on the way. ²⁹I know that when I come to you, I will come in the full measure of the blessing of Christ.

³⁰I urge you, brothers and sisters, by our Lord Jesus Christ and by the love of the Spirit, to join me in my struggle by praying to God for me. ³¹Pray that I may be kept safe from the unbelievers in Judea and that the contribution I take to Jerusalem may be favorably received by the Lord's people there, ³²so that I may come to you with joy, by God's will, and in your company be refreshed. ³³The God of peace be with you all. Amen.

I've deliberately left running narrative out of Romans 15 so you can look it over yourself and see how much of it lacks harmony to the Teachings of God and Jesus. Go back and review comments on what Paul said previously, especially chapters 5-8. Should you find I've misrepresented anything herein – drop me an email! I'm always open to learn as long as I'm able. richard@onedisipletoanother.org From my perspective there is no possibility that Paul handled the Holy Scripture uprightly in all his accounts. There is ample evidence he directly misrepresented the words of God and the Teachings of Yeshua. God does not elect who is saved and who is unsaved. Each person is responsible for themselves to Him. This is why Yeshua warned to "be careful who you hear", because "blind leaders of the blind will both fall into the ditch." It is indeed time to discover that we have "inherited falsehoods" that are useless to accomplish the fact that the Spirit works with the word of God to accomplish what God gave His instructions in righteousness to accomplish – that we are wise to the pathway of life God gave – and thereby know who speaks according to His everlasting Covenant – and who does not. Yeshua came to renew the Everlasting Covenant and to show the Gentiles it is HONORABLE to keep the Decrees of God! Yeshua came to call us from iniquity to then do what God decreed just and right, or sin, evil and abominations. All things are not lawful – God said so; Yeshua said so, and so did all the true prophets of God. Believers in Judea, who had the Hebrew Gospel of Matthew, were those who knew the Torah and the Teachings of Yeshua.

Footnotes

w. Romans 15:3 Psalm 69:9

x. Romans 15:8 Greek *circumcision*

y. Romans 15:9 2 Samuel 22:50; Psalm 18:49

z. Romans 15:10 Deut. 32:43

aa. Romans 15:11 Psalm 117:1

bb. Romans 15:12 Isaiah 11:10 (see Septuagint)

cc. Romans 15:21 Isaiah 52:15 (see Septuagint)

ROMANS 16
Personal Greetings

¹I commend to you our sister Phoebe, a deacon[a][b] of the church in Cenchreae. ²I ask you to receive her in the Lord in a way worthy of his people and to give her any help she may need from you, for she has been the benefactor of many people, including me. ³Greet Priscilla[c] and Aquila, my co-workers in Christ Jesus. ⁴They risked their lives for me. Not only I but all the churches of the Gentiles are grateful to them. ⁵Greet also the church that meets at their house. Greet my dear friend Epenetus, who was the first convert to Christ in the province of Asia. ⁶Greet Mary, who worked very hard for you. ⁷Greet Andronicus and Junia, my fellow Jews who have been in prison with me. They are outstanding among[d] the apostles, and they were in Christ before I was.

The twelve apostles are named in Matthew, and there is no record of Andronicus or Junia – let alone Paul or Saul or Saulus.

⁸Greet Ampliatus, my dear friend in the Lord. ⁹Greet Urbanus, our co-worker in Christ, and my dear friend Stachys. ¹⁰Greet Apelles, whose fidelity to Christ has stood the test. Greet those who belong to the household of Aristobulus. ¹¹Greet Herodion, my fellow Jew. Greet those in the household of Narcissus who are in the Lord.

See the link on Paul being related to the Herodians, which can be found in topical articles at: http:// jesuswordsonly.com/

The Herodians were not Jews.

¹²Greet Tryphena and Tryphosa, those women who work hard in the Lord.

Greet my dear friend Persis, another woman who has worked very hard in the Lord. ¹³Greet Rufus, chosen in the Lord, and his mother, who has been a mother to me, too. ¹⁴Greet Asyncritus, Phlegon, Hermes, Patrobas, Hermas and the other brothers and sisters with them. ¹⁵Greet Philologus, Julia, Nereus and his sister, and Olympas and all the Lord's people who are with them. ¹⁶Greet one another with a holy kiss. All the churches of Christ send greetings.

¹⁷I urge you, brothers, and sisters, to watch out for those who cause divisions and put obstacles in your way that are contrary to the teaching you have learned. Keep away from them. ¹⁸For such people are not serving our Lord Christ, but their own appetites. By smooth talk and flattery, they deceive the minds of naive people. ¹⁹Everyone has heard about your obedience, so I rejoice because of you; but I want you to be wise about what is good, and innocent about what is evil.

Balderdash. It is shown it was Paul who taught a gospel NOT in accord with the records given by the disciples of Jesus in Matthew. In fact, the "gospel" of Paul is not in accord with the Torah, Psalms or Prophets either. This is written that all seekers of truth will be enabled to see through the lies of Paul and be able to see the truth is that God has grace towards those who repent and turn to Him wholeheartedly and faithfully abide in His word and the Teachings of Master Yeshua – the one prophesied of in Genesis 49:10 to be the one to whom the "rule" belongs – attested to by God through his teachings, miracles, fulfillment of prophecy, giving true prophecy, and ascension to the throne on the right hand of God. Yeshua taught freedom to love and obey God and live a just and righteous life that will bring God the glory – Paul taught freedom from the Law and that the Law was a curse, the letter of the Law kills, and that God will hold the righteous accountable to pay the debt of sinners who will not live by the Instruction of God – but by imagined "spirit" without the clear, reliable, everlasting and true words of God Almighty.

[20]The God of peace will soon crush Satan under your feet. The grace of our Lord Jesus be with you. [21]Timothy, my co-worker, sends his greetings to you, as do Lucius, Jason and Sosipater, my fellow Jews. [22]I, Tertius, who wrote down this letter, greet you in the Lord. [23]Gaius, whose hospitality I and the whole church here enjoy, sends you his greetings. Erastus, who is the city's director of public works, and our brother Quartus send you their greetings. [24] [e]

[25]Now to him who is able to establish you in accordance with my gospel, the message I proclaim about Jesus Christ, in keeping with the revelation of the mystery hidden for long ages past, [26]but now revealed and made known through the prophetic writings by the command of the eternal God, so that all the Gentiles might come to the obedience that comes from[f] faith— [27]to the only wise God be glory forever through Jesus Christ! Amen.

God gave the Torah to Jew and Gentile at the same time. Yeshua commanded the same teachings given in Matthew to be given to men of all nations. Yeshua said all things had to be fulfilled in the Law and Prophets. We can now know we have inherited lies in the "Christian Bible", and it is time to repent and return to the pathway God gave for those who claim Him as their God – those who call upon His NAME.

Footnotes

dd. Romans 16:1 Or *servant*

ee. Romans 16:1 The word deacon refers here to a Christian designated to serve with the overseers/elders of the church in a variety of ways; similarly in Phil. 1:1 and 1 Tim. 3:8,12.

ff. Romans 16:3 Greek *Prisca*, a variant of *Priscilla*

gg. Romans 16:7 Or *are esteemed by*

hh. Romans 16:24 Some manuscripts include here *May the grace of our Lord Jesus Christ be with all of you. Amen.*

ii. Romans 16:26 Or *that is*

Jeremiah 16:19

"O LORD, my strength, and my fortress, and my refuge in the day of affliction, the Gentiles shall come unto thee from the ends of the earth, and shall say, **Surely our fathers have inherited lies, vanity, and wherein *is* no profit.**"

Surely this is because none of the Roman or Protestant reformers bothered to follow the words of God to make sure writings, they put in the New Testament were in accord with the words of God, as were the Teachings of Yeshua (Jesus). (Deut. 4, 12, 13, 18)

Hebrew Gospel of Matthew

CHAPTER 4

1. Then Yeshua was taken by the Holy Spirit into the wilderness to be tempted by Satan ("Satan" means "the accuser."

2. 2. He fasted forty days and forty nights and afterwards was hungry. [Satan means "accuser." Those who accuse falsely are satans.]

3. The tempter drew near and said to him: if you are the Son of God say that these stones should turn into bread. [Israel was called "son" of God, and "the" son would be the unique "that prophet" of Deut. 18 and Isaiah 42.]

4. Yeshua answered and said to him: It is written: not by bread alone, etc. [Here we see the text was cut short by Shem-Tob – for the sake of continuing the narrative the AENT is supplied: "It is written that the son of man does not live by bread alone, but by all the Words that proceed from the mouth of Elohim." Deut. 8:3. We should note that after the "fall", God informed Cain that he would be forgiven (elevated) by improving himself – not by blood sacrifice. The whole "fallen man" as incapable to do good or find favor with God by improving himself defies these words of God. Babies are not sinners. Men who refuse to obey God are. "Son of man" means to be a mortal – not God in the flesh.]]

5. Then Satan took him to the holy city, placed him on the highest point in all the temple

6. And said to him: If you are God, jump down, for it is written: he has commanded his angels in regard to you to keep you in all your ways, etc. [[It appears Shem-Tob was having issue to even copy the foundational Teachings as it existed in the Hebrew Matthew – again he cuts it short – and even inserted the idea of "if you are God", which was never claimed by Yeshua or Psalm 91:11-12 – but was claimed by Paul and his disciples who hi-jacked the faith as taught by Yeshua. This is one to be careful with the words of God that one does not pit one of His instructions against another. The point is to be within the parameters of the word of God that we not live outside His instruction and declaration. For the sake of continuing the narrative of his teachings, the AENT is supplied to maintain the Testimony of Yeshua:] …6. And said to him, "If you are the son of Elohim, cast yourself down for it is written that his Messengers he commands concerning you, and upon their hands they will bear you up that your foot should not strike upon a rock.]] [[[DSSB Psalm 91:11-12; "For he will give orders to his angels concerning you, to guard you in all your ways. In their hands they will lift you up, so that you do not strike your foot against a stone."]]] [[[[I've personally experienced a number of times when it

must have been angels who protected me, and untold numbers of people have had similar experiences. Since this is an obvious matter to many who have experienced it, the charge or challange by Satan seems hollow in two regards - it was not just for the singular "that prophet", or "unique" son of God (of Abraham, Isaac and Jacob), and it would certainly be folly to jump off a building to "prove God true to His promises" - which is why Jesus commented on not tempting God to keep His word. YHWH is not one to play truth or dare with. The only "test" we should do is to make His Covenant Decrees to be our Standard for life and then realize the Teachings of YHWH are true and are the means by which He will regard us true to Him and thereby be blessed eternally. This is what the Isaiah 56 passage is also about, as its roots trace back to Adam and Eve, Cain, Noah, Abraham, Isaac, Jacob, Moses and Mount Sinai. This also proves Jesus was teaching to obey the Father and the Covenant. Notice the Jewish account altered this to pretend it was something to prove "Christianity" was a lie - but the words of Jesus, as recorded by his disciples and the Holy Scriptures of support, prove their claim to be a lie.]]]]

7. Yeshua answered him again: You shall not tempt the Lord your God. [Deut. 6:16]

8. So Satan took him to an exceedingly high mountain, showed him all the kingdoms of the earth and their glory

9. And said to him: All these things I will give to you if you bare your head to me. [submit to Satan's ways of twisting the Teachings of God or defying the Teachings of God.]

10. Then Yeshua answered him: Go Satan, that is Satanas, for it is written: "I will pray to the Lord and him only you will serve. [[Again, questionable account by Shem-Tob, so the AENT is supplied: **Then Y'shua said to him "Leave enemy, for it is written that you will worship Master YHWH your Elohim and Him alone you will serve."** Deut. 6:13 and Exodus 20 and "V".]] [[[Note when Israel started invoking demons, even in the Temple, and sacrifice of their children.]]]

11. Then Satan left him and behold angels drew near to him and ministered to him.

12. It came to pass in those days Yeshua heard that John had been delivered up to prison, so he went into Gilgal.

13. He passed by Nazeral and dwelt in Capernaum-Raithah, that is Maritima, on the outskirts of the Land of Zebulun.

14. In order to fulfill that which Isaiah the Prophet said:

15. Land of Zebulun and land of Naphtali, the way of the Sea, beyond the Jordon, Galilee of the gentiles.

16. The people who walk in darkness have seen a great light, those who dwell in the land of deep darkness a light has shined upon them. [Isaiah 9:1 (8:23) 9:3 (9:2) 9:10] Some Jews claim Yeshua only went to the Jews, but this proves early on that he went to the Gentiles. Isaiah 42 also speaks of one who was to be a light to the Gentiles to show them it is honorable to keep the Torah (instruction in righteousness) of God – of which the Ten Declarations were given for all men – as were the standards of right and wrong; justice and mercy; knowing who He shows kindness towards (My people VS My enemies) and knowing what God declared Holy VS common. It appears to me that the whole "7 Noahite Law" is a fabrication of the "Oral Torah", as are the "613 Commandments", as YHWH declared the Ten Decrees are the Covenant.]]

17. Henceforth Yeshua began to preach and to say: Repent for the kingdom of heaven is near. [God was to be their King, but Israel spurned God and wanted an earthly king as the other nations. God had told them His Kingdom was near them – not some distant place – if they would simply and faithfully seek to do His will, as did Abraham – recall the words of God on this vital point: Psalm 91 and "The Valediction of Moses". There is no need to bother with the twisting of Romans 10:8 that "all have sinned and fallen short of the glory of God", as God said no such thing. As Paul quoted Isaiah, he was denying or totally ignorant of the Truth spoken of in the first chapter of Isaiah. Jewish folk should look into the alterations of the words throughout Isaiah evidenced as the DSSB footnotes – over 1000 changes!? I've heard scholars working on the DSS that it may take 300 years to complete. The obvious truths in the Decrees of God and the supporting passages that give further definition of His Teachings that include what He said is just restitution are not too hard to understand or do, and it is these matters that need to be restored to us that we live according to His Teachings and Decrees. (that we might "live justly, love mercy, and walk humbly with our God - YHWH. Also carefully note the words of God through Isaiah 56 and 57 of the core truth in Exodus and "V".]

18. Yeshua went along the shore of the sea of Galilee and saw two brothers, Shimon, who is called Simon, also called Petros, and Andrea his brother casting their nets into the sea because they were fishermen. [Acts, written by Luke, the personal biographer of Saul/Paul, testifies to the selection of the apostles to require they were with him from the beginning of his ministry, but Matthew, as written by them – testifies the Luke account is not accurate – hence one clue to not place the testimony of Luke on par with the testimony of Matthew. Luke is second and third hand testimony at best – and per the Instruction of God should not be equated to be true "Testimony" of Yeshua by his personally chosen disciples. (see the Instructions of God about witness testimony, as well as His Teachings to determine a true prophet from a false prophet (Deut. 4, 12, 13,18, and 34]

19. He said to them come after me and I will make you fish for men. (prophecy of fishing for men fulfilled? Jeremiah 16:16; Ezekiel 49:10) [Since they had Y'shua killed, note his prophecies of the coming king and kingdom. This is also foretold in Micah that "after those days" when Yeshua came to them, that there would be another scattering of Israel to the nations (diaspora is now nearing 2000 years of unrepentance).]

20. So they left their nets in that hour and went after him.

21. He turned from there and saw two other brothers, James and John, brothers who were sons of Zebedeel, that is Zabadao and Zabadah, and their father in a boat setting up their nets and he called them.

22. They hastened and left their nets and their father and followed after him.

23. Then Yeshua went around the land of Galilee teaching their assemblies and preaching to them the good gift, that is, mavangeleo, of the kingdom of heaven and healing all the sick and every disease among the people. [Note Isaiah 53 is about his work of healing the people - review the Hebrew translations. His bearing their sins was a load upon him, not that he was taking their sins upon himself to relieve them of their sinfulness! Note Isaiah 1 and Ezekiel 18, as well as the word of YHWH in the Covenant prove that "Jesus" was not taking the sins of the wicked upon himself so the wicked could then be declared righteous! How can such a belief of substitutionary righteousness be from YHWH or Yeshua or any true prophet of God? "If they do not speak according to the Law and the Testimony, there is no light in them."][[If people can change their lives because Jesus taught to abandon evil and learn to do good so men would praise God, why must they imagine the only reason God has grace towards anyone is based on being "covered by the blood of Jesus"? All need to grasp that the economy of God requires that repenting to Him preceeds forgiveness. Where in all the Holy Scripture do we find God forgives anyone of their sin when they are still in rebellion against doing what He declared good? (The Ten Decrees). It is far past time that the Covenant, as taught by God, the Prophets and That Prophet be taught to all who claim the Father in Heaven as their God. Paul defamed what God called good, and therefore must be rejected if we believe God or any true prophet of God.]]

24. So a report about him went into all the land Syria and they brought unto him all those who were sick from various kinds of deceases, those possessed by demons, those who were terrified by an evil spirit and those who shook, and he healed them. [Yeshua did more works than all the previous prophets of God – God proving He was with Yeshua in healing physical decease, demon possession, control over nature, raising the dead, and raising Yeshua from the dead, and finally, his ascending to the Ancient of Days as he prophesied he would – the claim he made

later in Matthew that the Jews considered blasphemy and who gathered false witnesses to say he claimed to be the Son of God – in Matthew was said to be the false charge. Yeshua came to call us from iniquity to do the will of God, which is why he emphasized his Teachings being from God, - Isaiah 42. Pay very close attention to this – did Yeshua teach the need for faithfulness to God through living rightly as God taught and instructed – or did he teach the Law was done away with because He fulfilled it and became to once for all human sacrifice to pay the price of sin for all men? (Doing the works of God, or faith alone/grace alone merely by belief in the gospel of the Cross according to Paul?)]

25. Many followed him from Kapoli and Galilee, from Jerusalem, Juda, and across the Jordan.

Supporting passages for teachings in Chapter 5 to show his teachings are according to the Torah, Psalms and Prophets. Another Dead Sea Scroll evidence: 4Q521; Messianic Apocalypse. [the heavens and the earth will listen to His Messiah, and none therein will stray from the commandments of the holy ones. Seekers of the Lord, strengthen yourselves in His service! All you hopeful in heart, will you not find the Lord in this? For the Lord will consider the pious and call the righteous by name. Over the poor His spirit will hover and will renew the faithful with His power. And He will glorify the pious on the throne of the eternal Kingdom. He who liberates the captives, restores sight to the blind, straightens the bent and forever I will cleave to the hopeful and in His mercy. And the fruit ... will not be delayed for anyone. And the Lord will accomplish glorious things which have never been as he.... For He will heal the wounded and revive the dead and bring good news to the poor. ... He will lead the uprooted and knowledge.... and smoke. Also see Isaiah 61:1,2, and the dialogue with the disciples of John the Baptist who were sent to Jesus while John was in jail - "are you the one"? Evidently not all the prophets writings made it into our current Bibles.

CHAPTER 5
The Sermon on the Mount

1. It came to pass after this when he saw the crowds that he went upon the mountain and sat down. Then his disciples (came to) him

2. And he opened his mouth and spoke to them saying:

3. Blessed are the humble of spirit for theirs is the kingdom of heaven. Is. 57:15; 66:2

4. Blessed are those who wait for they shall be comforted. Is. 66:2; 66: 10-12

5. Blessed are the meek for they shall inherit the earth. Ps. 37:11; 149:4

6. [missing – AENT supplied]: Blessed are they who hunger and thirst for righteousness because they will be satisfied. Ze. 2:3; Ps. 11:3-7; Is 56:1-8; 66:11-12.

7. [missing – AENT supplied]: Blessed are they who are merciful because mercies will be upon them. Ps. 18:25; 2 Sa. 22:6.

8. Blessed are the innocent of heart, for they shall see God. (This is perhaps the greatest hope we can have for those who came before us, or who had no way to know they had been told to believe in lies against God or His anointed one, Jesus/Joshua. To have an innocent heart one must become as a little child, as Jesus taught and exampled later. Those who have hidden the Teachings of Elohim from everyone cannot have an "innocent heart", but more likely a self-worshipping heart. This is most easily seen in the writings of the Prophets, such as Isaiah, that he was dealing with very evil people who claimed to be serving God. As Jesus absolutely taught take care, lest you be deceived.]] [[Those of Rabbinical Judaism have two "Torah's", their altered version, and the "oral torah" that is based on perversion of the Teachings of God. They don't want you to ever realize when they say "Torah", you have no way to know they may well be speaking of their own "oral torah" and not the record as given by Elohim/YHWH through Moses, or the altered record of what Elohim had spoken at Mount Sinai. Beware all of Judaism, but be innocent of heart towards God and your fellow man.]]

9. Blessed are those who pursue peace for they shall be called sons of God. Is. 26:12; Ps:122:8; 72:3-7.

10. Blessed are those who are persecuted for righteousness for theirs is the kingdom of heaven. Ps.38:20; Is. 66:5

11. Blessed are you when they persecute and revile you and say against you all kinds of evil for my sake, but speak falsely. Ps. 119:85-87; La. 3:22-23.

12. Rejoice and be glad for your reward is very great in heaven, for thus they persecuted the prophets. Ps. 37; 89:19-29. [Review historical record in the entire OT to verify that God was calling them to repent and live righteously – according to His instruction.]

13. At that time Jesus said to his disciples: You are salt in the world. If the salt is neutralized in regard to its taste with what will it be salted? It is fit for nothing but to be cast outside to be trampled under foot. Ps. 18; 37.

14. You are light in the world. A city built upon a hill cannot be hidden.

15. They do not light a lamp to place it in a hidden place where it cannot shine; but they place it upon a lamp stand so that it might shine for all in the house.

16. Thus let your light shine before every man to show them your good deeds which are praised and glorified before your Father who is in heaven. Ex. 10-20. [Consider the righteous until Abram were not "Jews" or "Israel", but men who feared God and lived circumspect lives in faithfulness to Him and teaching their children the pathways given by God. It was not until Jesus (Yeshua) that we find the call to make disciples of His pathways as taught in Matthew – which was soon overshadowed and confused by alteration of and addition to what Christians call the "New Testament" – a term curiously used by the first heretic – Marcion.] [[All three Abrahamic faith divisions divide over who Jesus was – then further divisions were introduced by Saul/Paul and alterations to Matthew and putting three other gospel accounts after Matthew that disagree with the testimony of Jesus' disciples who had written Matthew in Hebrew before 40 CE. The "Christian" "New Testament" is not the different word of God.]]

17. At that time Jesus said to his disciples: Do not think that I came to annul the Torah, but to fulfill it. Du. 4, 12, 13, 18, 34. Lev. Gen. Num. Ex. Nu. *Exodus 20; Is 42.

18. Truly I say to you that until heaven and earth depart not one letter or dot shall be abolished from the Torah or the Prophets, because all will be fulfilled. [[Ps. 89; Torah established as an eternal and everlasting covenant – Genesis through Deuteronomy. See the link on the Gospel and the Law and the link on how God said to know truth from lies. The Core of the Torah are the Ten Declarations, the blessings, and the curses. Realize that our current scriptures have been altered. See "The Valediction of Moses" account of Deuteronomy.]].

19. He who shall transgress one word of these commandments and shall teach others, shall be called a vain person in the kingdom of heaven, but whoever upholds and teaches them shall be called great in the kingdom of heaven. **[[If the "Commandments" were altered before Jesus' days, we may find it interesting to pay attention and see if the newly discovered Valediction of**

Moses account will bring more light to know Jesus taught according to the Covenant as originally given? I find this very compelling evidence.]]

20. At that time Jesus said to his disciples: Truly I say to you, if your righteousness is not greater than the Pharisees and the sages, you shall not enter into the kingdom of heaven. [Jesus was not saying the Pharisees and Sages were righteous, as we see later his condemnation of their haughty and hypocritical lives and teachings.]

21. Have you not heard what was said to those of old: You shall not murder and whoever murders is guilty of a judgment of death? [[Exodus 20]]

22. But I say to you, he who angers his companion is guilty of judgment; he who calls his brother inferior shall be guilty of judgment before the congregation; he who calls him a fool is guilty of the fire of Gehenna. [The principle is what leads to sin, and to cut off the practice before we trespass. Note Jesus teachings about being angry without cause, as the aim is to not give cause for offence that could lead to murder among brothers, as was the case with Cain and Abel – to say we believe we have been offended and discuss it – work it out between parties, and if necessary to be established by witnesses when a brother is not being just, right, or fair. If we love God we will seek to keep His commandments and Everlasting Covenant - as well as the Teachings of God given through Jesus (Yeshua).] **[[Note the deleted Tenth Commandment: "Thou shalt not hate your brother in thy heart. I am Elohim, your god." Jesus, although not told of this commandment by the Pharisees or Sages, testified according to the unaltered Standards given by God, as preserved in "V". How did he know, except he was Anointed by Elohim to Teach it is honorable for all men to live by the Teachings/Instructions as originally given by Elohim? Also see "the blessings and the curses, which say not to desire what is another, and cursed is to lust after what is another, such as a wife. Being unjustly angry with another was to violate the Covenant of God as it was given.]]**

23. If you should offer your gift at the altar and remember that you have a quarrel with your companion and he is complaining about you because of this matter

24. Leave your gifts there before the altar and go to appease him first and afterwards offer your gifts. [[Later prophets warning that sacrifices were useless if they weren't living by His standards of justice and righteousness, which includes what God said is just restitution.]] [[[When the righteous uphold the Teachings and Truth of God to those who believe in the false apostles lies - telling the Truth has never been an evil - but instead is greatly blessed by God. See the Teaching of Jesus about those who are spoken of as evil by men because they testify the Truth of God and Jesus' Teachings.]]]

25. Then Jesus said to his disciples: See that you hasten to appease your enemy while you are walking with him in the way lest he deliver you to the judge and this judge delivers you to the servant to put you into prison.[Context is the Jewish court that met to take matters to the priests to decide a case, which would be binding is Torah instruction – their ruling would be as binding as the word of God. This practice seems to have been abandoned well before the Babylonian exile.]

26. Truly I say to you, you will not come out from there until the last piece of money is given. [In the Torah a vital principle of justice is restitution, restitution as Decreed by Elohim - His defined standard of justice eliminates injustice. Jesus did not pay for your sins. Jesus calls us to repent of sins and then live by the Teachings of Elohim, which includes restitution as commanded by God, before God declared: "And so he shall be forgiven." See Leviticus and the rest of the Torah and prophets. One might even note the teachings of Daniel to the non Jew about what he should do to be forgiven of evils done. Daniel didn't tell him to make a blood sacrifice! Start paying attention to the words of Elohim; stop believing those who lie against Him!!!!]]]

27. Again he said to them: You have heard what was said to those of long ago: You shall not commit adultery. [Exodus 20 and supporting passages in the Torah, Leviticus]

28. But I say to you that everyone who sees a woman and covets her has already committed adultery with her in his heart. [Law gave definition, and he was speaking of lusting after other men's wives. This appears somewhat altered. Look to the "Valediction" account for clarity. Per "V" to lust after the woman/wife of another is to violate the Covenant Standards, and surely, coveting or lusting leads to the sin of adultery - both are wrong according to Elohim.]

29. If your right (eye) seduces you, put it out and cast is from you. [severe repentance and prevention – No record that this was to be literally taken, but is an obvious over statement to make the point. First Century Christians didn't gouge out eyes or cut off hands, what record exists that the Jews did either? Where did Jesus say sin proceeds from? Hands, feet, mouth - or heart? (mind)]]

30. Also, if your hand seduces you, cut it off. It is better for you to suffer the loss of one of your limbs than all your body in Gehenna. [Severe repentance to be found living justly on the narrow pathway]

31. Again Jesus said to his disciples: You have heard what was said to those of long ago that everyone who leaves his wife and divorces her is to give her a bill of divorce.

32. And I say to you that everyone who leaves his wife is to give her a bill of divorce. But concerning adultery, he is the one who commits adultery and he who takes her

commits adultery. [Not giving a bill of divorce is to be not divorced but committing adultery – because the Torah of Elohim commanded the certificate be given – a matter of the Law of God given through Moses. Note other conditions for divorce given in the Torah – it cannot be that only one cause is legal – this would be taking away from His Instruction – double check the conditions therein and be enlightened to what God declared – He will uphold the unaltered word. Check the Hebrew account and the DSSB] [[Since Jesus taught "all will be fulfilled" of the Torah, Psalms and Prophets – and it has been proven and observed the words of God contained in the both the Jewish and Christian Bibles have been altered – all need to go back to ensure what God had said by Jesus' days in the DSSB records yet untranslated. What is sin per Lev. 18 and all the specific words of God in the Torah? Double check!]

33. Again you have heard what was said to those of long ago: You shall not swear by My name falsely, but you shall return to the Lord your oath. [Exodus 20 and supporting passages] ***Isaiah 66:1; Psalm 48:2; Ecclesiastes 5:4-5; also note the opening of the "Valediction" account and the Ten Teachings given by Elohim, as this teaching of Jesus show he was teaching the Truth of God, not alterations of Pharisees. This also relates to swearing in the NAME of God falsely, which is in the Ten Decrees, the blessings and the curses.]

34. But I say to you not to swear in vain in any matter, neither by heaven because it is the throne of God.

35. nor by earth because it is the footstool of his feet, nor by Jerusalem because it is the city of God, [Lev. 19:12; Deut. 23:23; Deut. 23:23; Is 66:1; Ps. 48:2]

36. nor by your head for you are not able to make one hair white or black.

37. But let your words be yes yes or no no. Everything in addition to this is evil. [Being true to your word is the pathway of God – be very careful what you say you will or will not do – honor your word, fully intending what you say you can do.] [Jesus forgave and prayed for Peter – the issue is repentance and then being true.](a principle related to being created in the image of God – which leads back to the creation in Gen.) [[This also relates to the fact that Pharisee "contingencies" to separate the justice of Elohim in heaven, as opposed to doing His will on earth, is a gross injustice to do in the "NAME" of Elohim, and may well be "swearing falsely in His name." Another matter is their teaching that non-Jews do not have a soul (not really human who is also created in the image of God and worthy to be among those He calls "My people"), as shown in the Pharisee "Law of the tent."]

38. Again you have heard what is said in the Torah: An eye for an eye, a tooth for a tooth. (Ex. 21:24; Lev. 24:20; Deut. 19:21) [Read all of Leviticus 19 as God enlightens what it means to "You shall be holy, for holy am I, YHWH your God.*******]

39. But I say to you, do not repay evil for evil; but he who smites your right cheek provide from him the left. [Lamentations 3:30. Turning the other cheek is about doing justly. See the supporting passage about turning the other cheek in Lamentations. The site link about how to tell truth from lies by the Covenant of God is the second link on the website. Read it and know what God considers justice, which requires we know good from evil. Current Jewish and Christian scriptures have been significantly altered. God decreed justice as eye for eye, tooth for tooth, in current records - and the major point is there is but one law for justice - not one for Jews and a different one for everyone else. Orthodox Judaism Oral Torah's defy those Teachings of Elohim Almighty.]

40. He who wishes to oppose you in judgment and to rob your shirt, leave to him your garment. [Deferring to the side of mercy in judgment?]

41. He who asks you to go with him a thousand steps, go with him two thousand.

42. To him who asks from you give and to him who wishes to borrow from you do not hold back. [Torah teaching of God] [Love of neighbor is as yourself – not above yourself. This goes back to John's instruction that if we have two shirts, we are able to give one to another who has none. An important side note is historical practices of lending at interest - was considered a mortal sin on the same plain as murder. So is charging interest beyond the seven-year cycle. God gave Commandments that Judaism has been leading the world to violate and steal the wealth of nations and individuals. Since their love of money is legendary, it would be fruitless to comment further, except to say that it was even considered a mortal sin by the Catholic Church for over 1000 years - both Jews and Catholics led the way to situational ethics to turn the mortal sin into a sin that now is not. What did God say? That is what matters. Lending at interest was prohibited by God, perhaps only excepting the enemies of the faithful sons of God - which they obviously have not been for perhaps 3000 years? and at least 2000 years since they justified their hatred of Jesus. (Pharisees)]

43. Again Jesus said to his disciples: You have heard what was said to those of long ago that you shall love the one who loves you and hate the one who hates you.

44. But I say to you, love your enemies and do good to the one who hates you and vexes you and pray for those who persecute you and oppress you [Note how faithful Abraham petitioned God about His destroying Sodom if he could find but five righteous there. This does not say we have no right to defend ourselves from oppressors, but Jesus did warn that those who live by the sword will die by the sword - God does condone self-defense and justified war, as the Law gives instructions about both.]

45. in order that you might be sons of your father who is in heaven who causes his sun to shine of the good and evil and causes it to rain on the bad and the just. [In review of the Torah the principle was just restitution – not actually knocking out teeth "Just" being what God had declared to be just, not what we imagine and not what others might twist it into, but what can be clearly observed to be within the just restitution of handling the words of God uprightly Matters of going the second mile or giving our shirt might be examples of doing what God has required of man in "loving mercy" in Micah 6:7-8 – not just living by the letter of the Law that we might demand.] [[Later distinction is made – they were to go from town-to-town preaching, but if they were not received – if their peace was not returned to them – that they were to shake the dust off their feet as testimony against them – the principle is of peace first, but not obligated to endure those who reject their peace. Regarding "The Seven Noahite Laws", these are Rabbinical law, not the Law of Elohim. Some reasonably claim that these Seven Noahite Laws justify killing Christians when Judaic are in control. They are the ones who came up with that evil - not Elohim - and they expose their anti-humanity by belief in such things. Such ideas reject the Teachings Elohim gave to them. To see how far they have fallen in Orthodox Zionism from what Elohim had told them - shows the reason for "the time of Jacob's trouble" to by justified by Elohim against them.]]

46. If you love those who love you what is your reward? Do not the impudent love those who love them?

47. [Missing – AENT supplied]: And if you greet in peace only your brothers, what more are you doing? Do not even the publicans do this? *[new info. Due to the differences between the Covenant Decrees as originally given, more clarity can be observed than previous to the publication of "V", the Valediction of Moses. Pharisee teachings obscured those Teachings of Elohim, but the Teachings of Jesus give more clarity to them. The "publicans" were among the most hypocritical, as can be observed through the oral torah teachings of Judaism today. God made things simple, men complicated His Teachings. For example not the original Sabbath Teaching in "V", and compare that to the 700 plus pages of Pharisee Judaism's instructions they have given about how to keep the Sabbath (MISHNAH BERURAH). The Standards given by Elohim center on preservation of life and living justly and loving God and our fellow man, and being content with what we have and not desiring what another has, or become unjust by hating a brother in our heart.]] [[Where did God ever condone the viewpoint to do what is right in you own heart? When we live by His Covenant, truth, justice and mercy have definition and parameters.]] [[[[Also recall Jesus teaching that if our peace is not returned to us, that we are to dust off our feet as a testimony against them]]]] [*When Abraham negotiated with God on behalf of Sodom to find a few righteous within the city – he was not greeting them as brethren, but petitioning for their good – even

his sons-in-law failed the test to be righteous and chose to stand in the pathway of destruction.] " Know today and keep his decrees and commandments, so that it may go well for you and so that you may live long upon the land that Elohim, your god is giving you. Listen, Israel: Elohim, our god, is a single god. So love Elohim, your god, with all your heart and all your soul, very much, and keep these proclamations that I command you today upon your heart. Teach them to all your children and recite them when you sit at home, when you go on your way, when you lie down, and when you rise. Tie them as a declaration upon your arm, and they shall serve as an affirmation between your eyes. Inscribe them upon the posts of your home and gate. For Elohim made a pact with you at Horeb on the day of the assembly. I stood between Elohim and you at this time - for you were afraid on account of the fire and did not climb the mountain - to tell you the word of your god, as follows: (consolidated listing). *I am Elohim, your god, who freed you from the land of Egypt, from the slave-house. You shall not have any other gods. You shall not make a carving or any image that is in the heavens above or the earth below or in the waters beneath the earth. You shall not prostrate yourselves before them, and you shall not serve them. I am Elohim, your god. Blessed is the man who has Elohim as his god, and who* prostrates himself only to him, and who serves him alone. Cursed is the man who does a carving or a casting, the handiwork of a craftsman.

Sanctify the seventh day and rest on it. For in six days I made the heavens and the earth and all that is in them, and I rested on the seventh day. Therefore you too shall rest, along with your livestock and all that you have. I am Elohim, your god. Blessed is the man who sanctifies the seventh day and rests on it. Cursed is the man who does work on the seventh day.

Honor your father and your mother. I am Elohim, your god. Blessed is he who honors his father and his mother. Cursed is he who disgraces his father and mother.

You shall not slay the soul of your brother. I am Elohim, your god. Blessed is the man who does not avenge or exact retribution for the soul of his brother. Cursed is he who strikes down his fellow in secret.

You shall not commit adultery with the woman of your fellow. I am Elohim, your god. Blessed is the man who does not defile the woman of his fellow. Cursed is the man who approaches any of his kin, or who commits adultery with the woman of his fellow, or who copulates with any animal.

You shall not steal the property of your brother. I am Elohim, your god. Blessed is the man who does not cheat his fellow. Cursed is he who moves the boundary marker of his fellow.

You shall not swear in my name falsely (or to deceive), for I shall avenge the transgression of the fathers against the sons, grandsons, and great grandsons for those who bear my name falsely. I am Elohim, your god. Blessed is the man who does not swear in my name falsely. Cursed is the man who swears falsely in my name.

You shall not submit against your fellow a false judgment. I am Elohim, your god. Blessed is the man who does not deceive or lie to his fellow. Cursed is he who takes a bribe to give false judgment against his comrade.

You shall not desire the woman of your fellow, his male servant, his female servant, or anything that is his. I am Elohim, your god. Blessed is he who does not lust after anyone belonging to his fellow. Cursed is the man who desires and lusts after the woman of his fellow, his daughter, his female servant, or anything that is his.

You shall not hate your brother in your heart. I am Elohim, your god. Blessed is the man who loves his fellow. Cursed is the man who hates his brother in his heart.

It is these ten pronouncements that Elohim uttered to you upon the mountain from amid the fire. Blessed is the man who upholds all the proclamations of this teaching to perform them. Cursed is the man who does not uphold all the proclamations of this teaching to perform them.

48. Be you (perfect) as your father is perfect. [passages associated with Ex. 20 and **Lev. 19. Don't be deceived by the writings of Saul/Paul, or his disciples, who mischaracterized the Standards Elohim gave us to live by. As Jesus taught, live by the Standards given by Elohim, not Orthodox Rabbi, or the fake apostle Paul. Seek and ye shall find - but seek the most original Testimony - Jews even altered the Ten Decrees of God, so let's be honest with God, according to His words of life, not the lies of those following Satan, who alter and lie about what Elohim said.]

Supporting passages for teachings in Chapter 5 to show his teachings are according to the Torah, Psalms and Prophets.

Chapter 6

1. Beware lest you do your righteousness before men that they might praise you; if you do, you will have no reward from your father who is in heaven.

2. Again Jesus said to them; When you do righteousness do not wish to make a proclamation or sound trumpets before you as the hypocrites, that is, Hippocrates, who do their righteousness in the streets and in the marketplaces in order that men might see them. Truly I say to you, they have received their reward already.

3. But you when you do righteousness, let not your left hand know what your right hand is doing,

4. in order that your gift might be in secret and your father who sees hidden things will reward you.

5. At that time Jesus said to his disciples: When you pray do not raise your voice and do not be like the sad hypocrites who love to pray in the synagogues and in the corner of the courtyards and pray with haughty speech that men might hear and praise them. Truly I say to you, they have received their reward already.

6. But you, when you pray, go to your couch, close your doors upon you, and pray to your father in secret, and your father who sees in secret will reward you.

7. So you, when you pray, do not multiply words as the heretics who think that by the multitude of words they will make them heard.

8. Do you not see that your father who is in heaven knows your words before you ask from him?'

9. But thus you shall pray: Our father, may your name be sanctified.

10. May your kingdom be blessed; may your will be done in heaven and on earth. [Jesus taught defying the "contingencies" of the Pharisees, which is one reason they had him killed: because he said to obey Elohim, not man. Jesus taught what God, Moses, Joshua, and all the true prophets taught: cease doing evil and return to God and trust in His faithfulness to His words of life towards those He can call "My people."]

11. Give our bread continually.

12. Forgive us our sins as we forgive those who sin against us,

13. and do not lead us into the power of temptation but keep us from all evil, amen.

14. If you forgive men, their sins your father who is in heaven will forgive your sins. [Do recall the teachings of Jesus are to be in accord to the Standards given by Elohim, not against them. Per the Teachings of God in the Torah, forgiveness must be from the heart - not only in words alone.]

15. But if you do not forgive them, he will not forgive you your sins. [Note when God commanded sins to be forgiven and also consider when He said they weren't.]

16. Again he said to them: When you fast do not be as the sad hypocrites who make themselves appear sad and who change their faces to show their fasting before men; truly I say to you, they have received their reward already.

17. But you when you fast, wash your heads

18. that you might not appear to men to be fasting but (to) your father who is in secret, and your father who is in secret will reward you.

19. Again he said to them: Do not keep on heaping up treasures on earth so that decay and the grub devour it or thieves dig through and steal them.

20. Make for yourselves treasures in heaven where the worm and the grub do not devour them and where thieves do not dig through and steal. [The world to come was first spoken of in I Enoch and who will inherit it. Jews removed it from their Scripture because Christians were using it to defend their belief and faith in Jesus; Christians removed it because it testifies the world to come is attained by right of how they lived – not faith alone, or grace alone.]

21. In the place where your treasure is there will be your heart.

22. The lamp of your body is your eyes. If your eyes look straight ahead your body shall not be dark.

23. If your eyes grow dim your whole body will become dark and if the light which is in you becomes dark, all your ways will be dark. [Relates to reforming our life view to match what God said is living faithfully to Him – abiding in His word.]

24. At that time Jesus said to his disciples: No one is able to serve two masters except he hates the one and loves the other, or he honors the one and despises the other; you cannot serve God and the world. [Paul taught against God and Jesus; one cannot serve Paul and serve God. How can one believe someone who said the blessing of God is a curse? (Ten Decrees) How can one believe someone who said the Covenant Standards (Ten Decrees) were not even given by God, but by lowly angels as a curse to Israel? Awaken from the sleep the lies of Paul have placed over the real Teachings of Elohim. Repent to obey God indeed]

25. Therefore I say to you; do not be anxious for the food of your souls nor for the clothing for your body, because the soul is more precious than food and the body than clothing.

26. Behold the birds of the sky which sow nor reap nor gather into barns, but your exalted Father feeds them. Are you not more precious than they?

27. .Who among you of those who are anxious is able to add to his height one cubit?'

28. If this is the case, by are you anxious about clothes? Behold the lilies of Sharon, that is, "Gilyon," in sowing they neither spin nor weave.

29. But I say to you that King Solomon in all his glory was not clothed like these.

30. If God clothes the straw which is left in the standing grain, that is, pennon, which is fresh today and tomorrow is dried up and is placed into the oven, so much more will he clothe you who are little of faith.

31. If God so thinks of you, do not be anxious saying what shall we eat and what shall we drink, because all these things the bodies seek. But your Father knows that you need all these things.

32. Seek first the kingdom of God and his righteousness and all these things will be given to you.

33. Do not be anxious for tomorrow because tomorrow will be anxious for itself. Sufficient for itself is today with its trouble.

Chapter 7

1. Judge not let you be judged.

2. With what judgment you judge and with what measure you use, it will be measured to you. [God already gave standards for living and justice and commanded "My people" to live by them. In proper context, this teaching deals with judging by yours or another standards placed above what God Declared, in effect to either add to or take away from His given Commandments, ordinances, etc... To deny this principle would be to reject the Declarations and standards of Truth and Grace. Elohim gave proper criteria for judging in the Law details, especially noting Leviticus and His declaring "And so he shall be forgiven." This is the proper context of judging matters, to judge according to His Instructions. To teach God commanded, via Jesus, that we do not judge, lest we be judged, is not to be handling the words of Elohim uprightly. In some things Elohim allows and provides for mercy, and in some thing He doesn't. Study to show what would abiding in the words of Elohim requires we do, that we judge uprightly and according to His Teachings about Justice and Mercy. This is where Judaism first failed, pretending to judge on earth one way, but not be according to the Justice of God in Heaven. This directly relates to the "Lord's Prayer", that the will of God be done on earth as it is in heaven. Study of the "Oral Torah" shows many places where judgment is accepted on earth, but not from Elohim in heaven. This is why Jesus said we are to do things to where our 'yes' is yes, and our "no" is not - not a hodge-podge ad-hoc judicial system that is not in accord with the Instructions given by Elohim. It is also this principle that shows the current account of Jesus' teachings on divorce were altered.]

3. Why do you see the straw in the eye of the other person but not see the beam in your own eyes?

4. How is it that you say to the other person: Wait for me a while and I will cast the straw out of your eyes, and behold the beam in your own eyes? (If we cannot observe ourselves, to judge ourselves to be within "The Holy Way" of Isaiah 35, how can we judge others? Carefully study the Ten Decrees (original), and the "blessings and the curses" of Deuteronomy 11. Do what is right, keep from that which is evil.]

5. Hypocrite, first cast the beam out of your eyes and afterwards you will cast the straw out of the eye of your fellowman. [Don't be a hypocrite. This was a main fault of the Pharisees and sages of Jesus days, and as we can now see, the "scribes" were also in league with the Pharisees and sages to alter the Covenant, as proven in "V." (The Valediction of Moses).]

6. Again he said to them: Do not give holy flesh to dogs nor place your pearls before swine lest they chew them before you and turn to rend you. [This was not about telling people the truth of God and of their need to repent to observe and obey Elohim, as this is exactly what Jesus was doing throughout his entire ministry. However, regarding the real truth, if people do not accept the truth, and your peace is not returned to you, that is grounds to "shake the dust from your feet" as a testimony against them and to not bother with them anymore. As with Sodom, people are either righteous, or not.]

7. Ask from God and it will be given to you, seek and you will find, knock and it will be opened to you. [This has certainly proven true for my search for the "Original Jesus" who taught in accord with the Everlasting Covenant as given by Elohim at Mount Sinai and ratified by those of many nations who had left Egypt to serve the God of Abraham, Isaac and Jacob.]

8. Everyone who asks will receive, by the one who seeks it will be found, and to the one who calls it will be opened. [This is absolutely proven true, but not for those who are not seeking to be real with Elohim.]

9. Who is there among you whose son asks him for a piece of bread and he gives him a stone?

10. Or if he should ask for a fish, he gives him a snake?

11. But if you being evil come to place good gifts before yourselves, so much the more your father who is in heaven will give his good spirit to those who seek him.

12. . Everything you wish that men should do to you, do to them; this is the Torah and the words of the prophets. [This is the principle taught in the Torah and Prophets – since Jesus upheld every word of God and said to live by every word of God – this should not be twisted to think we can set aside what God said and then just do what we see expedient – God is Judge, and He already declared what His standards and judgments are – from the first of the Ten Declarations.] [[It may also be observed that other nations treatment of Israel during the Exodus and taking possession of the Land of Promise also examples their treatment of Israel that was then reflected back upon themselves. Since the Judgments and Love of God are required to be just and reciprocal, this judgement also stands against an unfaithful Israel, or the unfaithful Christian. God can forgive, but not those in active rebellion against Him or "My people." The Ten Teachings are the Standard for all those Elohim calls "My people." (Exodus and Isaiah 56, 57]]

13. At that time Jesus said to his disciples: Enter in the narrow gate because the gate of destruction is wide and deep, and many are going through it.

14. How narrow is the gate and grievous the way that leads straight to life and few are those who find it.

15. Again he said to them: Beware of false prophets who come to you in wool clothing like sheep, but inside are tearing wolves. [Beware false apostles and false teachers and fake gospels.]

16. By their deeds you will know them. Does a man gather grapes from thorns or figs from briars? [The following points of fruits is in context to what Elohim said regarding the fruits He was due. These are explicitly told in the Covenant Decrees, the Blessings and the Curses. Each are very clear and easy to understand. There should be no doubt by observations of the one doing, or the one observing what another does. Jesus was teaching to live life so that it will be blessed by God. Another Rabbi near Jesus time was Hillel, should you observe what Hillel taught, it is apparent he was seeing how close he could get to living a life that will not be cursed - but he had little in comparison to teaching to live a life that Elohim declared He will bless - this is a key element to understand when observing what Jesus had to say about the Pharisees and Rabbi of his day, and is why they were jealous and sought to do away with him. Recall at the end that the regular folks who were amazed at his teachings were not recorded to be amongst the group that were crying out 'Crucify him!' The main point herein is to also realize Isaiah 53 is talking about Jesus bearing their sicknesses, and in his unjust death - their ways of iniquity - not as a blood sacrifice for sins. Think about this as you read on. Observe.]

17. Every good tree makes good fruit and every bad tree makes bad fruit.

18. The good tree cannot make bad fruit, nor can the bad tree make good fruit.

19. Every tree which does not make good fruit is to be burned by fire. [Recall forever that the focus of the Covenant is to live justly, love mercy, and walk humbly with God, keeping in mind that Adam was created in the image of God, and upon that premise, is both capable and responsible to become what he was created to become. Truth has no part in lies. God never condoned or blessed those who ignored His Standards, to then live by whatsoever the individual who justifies themselves by justifying defying Him. Recall the Prophets spoke of those who each did what was right in their own eyes were falling backwards, not progressing in the pathway of life, or the ways of Elohim. What did God say? "Because thou hast rejected knowledge, I will also reject thee."]

20. Therefore it is according to fruits, that is, by their deeds, you will know them.

21. Because not everyone who says unto me, Lord, will enter the kingdom of heaven, but the one who does the will of my Father who is in heaven will enter the kingdom of heaven.

22. Many will say to me in that day, Lord, Lord, did we not prophesy in your name and in your name cast out demons and do many signs in your name.

23. Then I will say to them: I never knew you. Depart from me all you workers of iniquity. [those who were not living by the word of God] [Ps 6:8-9; Mt 7:21; 12:50] [[In the 160 CE Aramaic the Covenant standards of God, the Ten Decrees and directly associated reference passages were the point of knowing who is working iniquity, or not. If you think the Covenant Standards given by Elohim don't matter any more because Paul said so, you have to of necessity deny the testimony of God, all the Prophets and Psalms, as well as Joshua (Jesus).]]

24. Again he said to them: Everyone who hears these words and does them is like a wise man who built (his) house on a rock.

25. The rain came down against it and the winds beat it and it did not fall because its foundation was a rock.

26. Everyone who hears these my words and does not do them is like a foolish man who built his house upon the sand. [Scriptures noted are not inclusive, as many more might be noted throughout the Hebrew Scripture. It's about how we live life and our relationship to God and others. Rather than being little kernals of grain with no life in them, we are enabled by His instruction to become all we were created to be – now and forever. Elohim said, "Choose life that ye might live!" I'll be totally honest here - those who believe the Covenant of Elohim has passed away and reject considering it anymore - they have directly cursed themselves because they are rejecting the Standards Elohim gave mankind to live by! If this makes any sense to you - why not ask your Preacher or Priest to explain why they have taught you to reject what Jesus said we must to.]

27. The rains came down, the floods came and fell against it, (and it fell) with a great fall. [After years of being persecuted for telling the Truth of Elohim, know that if you do choose to believe God and choose to live a life He will bless - those of Satan will be true to their "god" and seek to destroy you for daring to believe and obey the One True God, and Orthodox and Zionist Judaism could be the proven core from which many evils on earth have found roots to. (Via many books written by their Sages - Talmuds, Zohar, Beginning of Wisdom, etc.)]]] [[If this is not true, then how is it that the charges against Joshua have multiplied from what they accused him of before they had him killed???? See: "Trial of the Ages" link. "King" is not an office appointed by the vote of the Rabbi - look at the records for Saul and David.]]

28. While Jesus was speaking these words all the people were greatly astonished at his conduct,

29. Because he was preaching to them with great power, not as the rest of the sages. [Dare to read the "Oral Torah" books of Orthodox Judaism. Then you will grasp what Joshua was teaching against; the teachings of men versus the Teachings of God is easily observed if we dare to put them side by side. In the age of deception, telling the truth is a crime worthy of death - that is what they did to Joshua (Jesus), and what they have in store for you, if you dare to observe the REAL TEACHINGS of Elohim. And it isn't just Orthodox Judaism, it is about all those who put Paul (who claimed to be a Pharisee), or any other man, on par with Elohim or Joshua. (Orthodox Judaism instructions on the Sabbath are not just to obey the teaching of God in the Decrees, but they turned it into 564 pages of their instructions in "The OHR OLAM Edition of the "MISHAN BERURAH.)]

Some books I've read for your consideration:

Jesus Words Only, Douglas DelTondo

Let's Get Biblical, Volumes 1 and 2, Tovia Singer

The Valediction of Moses, Idan Dershowitz

The Origins of Judaism, Jonatan Adler

The Moses Scroll, Ross Nichols

Multiple books by Robert Eisenman

Rabbinical Literature: or, The Traditions of the Jews, J.P. Stenelin

The Talmud Tested, Judaisms Strange Gods, Hoffman

The Dead Sea Scrolls Bible, Abegg, Flint, Ulrich

Hebrew to English translations: ETZ HYIM, JPS, Artscroll, Soncino volumes

The Hebrew Gospel of Matthew, George Howard

Aramaic English New Testament, Andrew Roth

One Disciple to Another – the Original Jesus, Richard Epler

Jewish Messiahs, Jerry Rabow

An Amazing Journey Into the Psychotic Mind - Breaking the Spell of the Ivory Tower - Jerry Marzinsky and Sherry Swiney

See chart at end for historical development of the New Testament Canon – Paul Harvey and Geoff Trowbridge.

Comments were largely based on the NIV, but the writings of Paul are based on the same accounts – look to other versions of Romans to see if the comments fit. The same basic message of the gospel of Paul can be known from any version.

I think the Marzinsky – Swiney book is needful to provide evidence and reason that exposes what we've heard about brain chemical imbalance and hearing voices has a very observable (by evidence) cause, effect, and the proposed solution is rejecting lies. Given the delusional mindset of many, how can we know we are not deceived? How to know who to listen to – may be the most critical skill we can learn from God. Don't be deceived – learn to know – KNOWING excels faith and belief. If you think this does not involve Christianity – open your ears to how many people are saying God, Jesus, or the Holy Spirit spoke to them. These claims fill the earth. Which are true? Which are not? When you hear a lie, simply declare: "That's a lie" – don't accept it.

Nazarenes 40 CE Hebrew Gospel of Matthew, Rejected 10 Pauline letters

Ebionites 40 CE Hebrew Gospel of Matthew, Rejected 10 Pauline letters

Elchesai 100 CE Hebrew Gospel of Matthew, Rejected 10 Pauline letters

Papias 130 CE Hebrew Gospel of Matthew and Mark

Marcion 140 CE First noted Christian heretic Accepted 10 Pauline letters

Marcion also had a modified Luke – very different – was it a proto-Luke?

Montanius 155 CE Accepted Gospel of John

Tatian 166 CE HGOM? Rejected Acts (was Acts before Luke?)

Alogi 170 CE Rejected Gospel of John

Iranaeus 180 CE Accepted Pauline letters, John, Mark, Hebrews, Revelation

Jerome 419 CE Accepted both HGOM and Greek Matthew and many books

Missing HGOM in accounts until 828 CE

Nicephonus 828 CE Rejected HGOM.

New Testament Canon may not have been officially declared until about the time of the printing press. First page of Onedisciptetoanother.org has a link to download the entire table by Geoff Trowbridge based on data from Paul Harvey. For historical perspective, Martin Luther did not think Revelation should be Scripture.

Observing and using common sense with the words of God.
(Open your mind to the words of God)

Consolidated account of the Decrees of Elohim from THE VALEDICTION OF MOSES, translated by Idan Dershowitz ("V") record of the Decrees, as of 3/21 (proto-Deuteronomy as it existed in the days near Ezekiel). (alternate translation of Ross Nichols in paranthasis) Recall also that it appears to be in the format of ancient Suzerainty Treaties used near the time of Abraham.

..."Be careful, lest you forget and make for yourselves a carving or image in the form of any figure that is in the heavens above or upon the earth below or in the waters beneath the earth. For my anger would then burn against you, and I would eradicate you swiftly from upon this good land. Know today and keep his decrees and commandments, so that it may go well for you and so that you may live long upon the land that Elohim, your god is giving you. Listen, Israel: Elohim, our god, is a single god. So love Elohim, your god, with all your heart and all your soul, very much, and keep these proclamations that I command you today upon your heart. Teach them to all your children and recite them when you sit at home, when you go on your way, when you lie down, and when you rise. Tie them as a declaration upon your arm, and they shall serve as an affirmation between your eyes. Inscribe them upon the posts of your home and gate. For Elohim made a pact with you at Horeb on the day of the assembly. I stood between Elohim and you at this time - for you were afraid on account of the fire and did not climb the mountain - to tell you the word of your god, as follows:

I am Elohim, your god, who freed you from the land of Egypt, from the slave-house. You shall not have any other gods. You shall not make a carving or any image that is in the heavens above or the earth below or in the waters beneath the earth. You shall not prostrate yourselves before them, and you shall not serve them. I am Elohim, your god. (Preamble in form of ancient Suzeraianty Treaty, followed by the Rules?)

Sanctify the seventh day and rest on it. For in six days I made the heavens and the earth and all that is in them, and I rested on the seventh day. Therefore you too shall rest, along with your livestock and all that you have. I am Elohim, your god. Blessed is the man who sanctifies the seventh day and rests on it. Cursed is the man who does work on the seventh day.

Honor your father and your mother. I am Elohim, your god. Blessed is he who honors his father and his mother. Cursed is he who disgraces his father and mother.

You shall not slay the soul of your brother. I am Elohim, your god. Blessed is the man who does not avenge or exact retribution for the soul of his brother. Cursed is he who strikes down his fellow in secret.

You shall not commit adultery with the woman of your fellow. I am Elohim, your god. Blessed is the man who does not defile the woman of his fellow. Cursed is the man who approaches any of his kin, or who commits adultery with the woman of his fellow, or who copulates with any animal.

You shall not steal the property (wealth) of your brother. I am Elohim, your god. Blessed is the man who does not cheat his fellow. Cursed is he who moves the boundary marker of his fellow.

You shall not swear in my name falsely (or to deceive), for I shall avenge the transgression of the fathers against the sons, grandsons, and great grandsons for those who bear my name falsely. I am Elohim, your god. Blessed is the man who does not swear in my name falsely. Cursed is the man who swears falsely in my name.

You shall not submit against your fellow a false judgment. I am Elohim, your god. Blessed is the man who does not deceive or lie to his fellow. Cursed is he who takes a bribe to give false judgment against his comrade.

You shall not desire the woman of your fellow, his male servant, his female servant, or anything that is his. I am Elohim, your god. Blessed is he who does not lust after anyone belonging to his fellow. Cursed is the man who desires and lusts after the woman of his fellow, his daughter, his female servant, or anything that is his.

You shall not hate your brother in your heart. I am Elohim, your god. Blessed is the man who loves his fellow. Cursed is the man who hates his brother in his heart.

It is these ten pronouncements that Elohim uttered to you upon the mountain from amid the fire. Blessed is the man who upholds all the proclamations of this teaching to perform them. Cursed is the man who does not uphold all the proclamations of this teaching to perform them.

How many different people are identified therein? Father, mother, brother, comrad and fellow, son, daughter, and servant (translated by Dershowitz as slave). God said there is one law for all, and that those around them should see this Law and good and praise Elohim for His goodness via the wisdom of the Law given to them. If each of the Standards are viewed only to a "brother", or "fellow", or "comrad" – and they were doing evils against those not explicitly as listed – who would be impressed at the wisdom to only treat some people fairly, and the rest were to be taken advantage of to lie, cheat, or in through any other means abuse your relationship to them because the Decree of God said, in your opinion, that it was OK to commit adultery, or whatever evil, against another – just because they didn't live close to you? Or that only men were to be considerate of others, and the women and children could be as lawless as the Rabbi deemed possible to do and still be faithful to God? The fact that God said there is but One Law for everyone means if we would not be doing such evils towards our fellow or neighbor or children – we should not be doing it to others either. This is the point made by Jesus throughout his teachings to show 'neighbor' had a broad meaning, and that being considerate and good to all, as reasonable and possible, is good, as the Father in Heaven is mindful of the welfare of all. (makes to rain on the just and unjust)

Elohim brought all out of Egypt who desired to believe and serve Him, and thereby to be blessed by Him, (carefully observe in Exodus that those of the multitude of nations who came to believe in Him and Moses due to observing He did as Moses said He would for those who were doing as He commanded the people to do to be under His protection.) to serve Him, both Israel and the multitude of nations were led and preserved by Him to Mount Sinai. Keeping His Covenant as given is to "serve God and keep His Commandments (Covenant.)" All the people were present together at Mount Sinai when the Covenant was spoken by Elohim and ratified by them all the same day! How could this not be the day Elohim spoke of to bless all the nations through the seed of Abraham, Isaac, and Jacob? (Note the accounts in Genesis wherein the source of this promise resides – do not confuse or obscure the record to cover up the plain truth.)

It is very telling of Rabbinical Judaism to note the differences between the Covenant record in "V" and the record we have in our currently published Bibles. There are many differences, starting with the outline given by Elohim in the opening Decree. Where in "V" do we find Elohim calling some to be His "enemies", as some current translations tell? Who are the enemies of God - what did He say? What did He say via the Prophets sent to Israel, or the records of Isaiah, Jeremiah, Daniel and Jonah, where a prophet was speaking to foreigners, not only Israel?

Evidence of "V" as compared to our texts will show many good reasons to observe "V" as the original Decree/Standard/Covenant He gave at Mount Sinai, which were evidently altered by those near the time of Ezekiel. The book of Ezekiel can also be observed to be out of chronological order, which can certainly effect seeing why Ezekiel was altered - to shift the rebuilding of the Temple in Ezekiel from the days after the Babylonian Captivity and their return, to a time in the future. It looks to me the matter is that they did not rebuild as God had instructed through Ezekiel, so they "kicked the can" down the road to some unknown date they could pretend to support? or feign hope in? That is between them and Elohim, but the historical evidence of what has happened to Israel since Ezekiel seems to show ample evidence they did not return with a "whole heart."

Was the Ark of the Covenant hidden so no one would discover "they" altered the Covenant written in stone? (I'm not speaking of our everyday Judaic here, but of the ancient leadership that has developed into what we can observe today as "Orthodox Judaism" and their "Oral Torah(s)" guidance from their "sages of blessed memory" from Babylon forward). We have the "Code of Hammurabi" stone, why not the records of the stone tablets written on by Elohim? For that matter, why have we not found record of them all over ancient Israel, to have been written on their doorposts and gates, or anywhere else?!

See the end of Genesis where the patriarch is pronouncing prophecy to his sons, as to whether their prophecy was true - what would become of them in the end. Also read "The Song of Moses," and see if Elohim is done with them, or not? Was Moses a true prophet of Elohim, or not? How has Elohim not been true to His word? Perhaps most important is to note what He said in the "V" account of the Cursed Decree.

Regarding the current account and "enemies" of God, the seventh, eighth, and tenth are where we find Elohim stating very important Standards/Teachings/Commandments:

(7) You shall not swear in my name falsely, for I shall avenge the transgression of the fathers against the sons, grandsons, and great grandsons for those who bear my name falsely. I am Elohim, your god.

(8) You shall not submit against your fellow a false judgment. I am Elohim, your god.

(10) You shall not hate your brother in your heart. I am Elohim, your god.

If Joshua (Jesus) was falsely accused by bribed witnesses, falsely condemned, and then politically forced Rome to crucify him - any action against his accusers could well be Elohim being true to His Covenant as given, not that those who altered His Covenant are blessed to continue in unrepented errors and teaching their children to add evil to evil, or injustice to injustice as they multiplied the charges against Jesus, and declared war upon all the followers of Jesus. Which other religion teaches hatred against Jesus? Which other religion teaches anyone not belonging to a certain genealogy (Jews) are no more than an animal with no soul or God-given sense? See "The Trial of the Ages" statements of why Orthodox Judaism believes Jesus to be the greatest false prophet in the history of Israel:

"All the Prophets foretold that the Messiah would redeem the Jews, help them, gather in the exiles and support their observance of the commandments. But he (Jesus) caused Jewry to be put to the sword, to be scattered and to be degraded; **he tampered with the Torah and its laws;** and he misled most of the world to serve something other than God" (Hil. Melachim 11:4)." **[As we should observe this day, they are the ones who tampered with the Torah – not Jesus.]**

"After that there arose <u>a new sect</u> which <u>combined the two methods, namely, conquest and controversy, into one</u>, because it believed that this procedure would be more effective in wiping out every trace of the Jewish nation and religion. It, therefore, resolved to lay claim to prophecy and to found a new faith, contrary to our Divine religion, and to contend that it was equally God-given. Thereby it hoped to raise doubts and to create confusion, since one is opposed to the other and both supposedly emanate from a Divine source, which would lead to the destruction of both religions. **For such is the remarkable plan contrived by a man who is envious and querulous. He will strive to kill his enemy and to save his own life, but when he finds it impossible to attain his objective, he will devise a scheme whereby they both will be slain.**"

"**The first one to have adopted this plan was Jesus the Nazarene, may his bones be ground to dust.**" (Quotes from Wikipedia, as of June 2020.)

[Those are the long-standing confession of evil minds, as they accused Jesus of what they had done, and in demanding all Jews submit to their rulings, rather than simply to hear and obey God and be faithful to the Covenant as given by Elohim] (Rabbinical judgments against Jews who do not uphold the Oral Torah's above the Torah of Elohim, or Jews who are not Zionist – both are condemned by Zionist Orthodox Judaism.) **Carefully note who the Zionist Orthodox Jews say are worthy to study their oral torah's – women, the poor, the unlearned, and the non-Jews are placed to a status near that of a simple animal – not a human being created in the image of Elohim. [see: The Talmud Tested; Judaism Discovered; Judaism's Strange Gods; The Secret Relationship Between Blacks and Jews, three volumes; and Synagogue of Satan. Within these books are adequate references to misguided "Oral Torah" beliefs of the rabbinical "sages".]**

Returning to the Covenant as given in "V"; there were three important matters that the people were to be taught: "The Covenant Statements of Elohim", "the blessings" and "the curses". The outline of life given by Elohim is He is our God, and that we are to serve Him only. As told through the prophets, we are to learn to "cease evil, and learn to do good," (Isaiah 1) and that we are to "do no evil."

This is where "The blessings and the curses" come into play for our benefit. If we are to first repent to "do no evil", the basic outline of good and evil are given in the "blessings and curses" - pay close attention to what Elohim said is blessed, and pay close attention to what Elohim said is cursed (evil?). These are His everlasting instructions. Each of those statements are easily seen and understood by anyone with a mind to live justly, love mercy, therefore being mindful of their relationship with fellow humanity being required to serve Elohim via keeping the Covenant. Rather than pretending the ultimate unforgivable sin is "blasphemy against the Holy Ghost", we need to realize that account in Matthew was likely added to foster prohibition from daring to compare the words of God to the "mysteries" and "revelations" taught by Paul - perhaps the greatest liar in human history, if the Standard for judgment are the easily known Teachings and Standards given in the Covenant of Elohim. Because of the depth Jesus taught of the Covenant, and his total grasp of it proving Elohim was directly inspiring him is shown in the fact that the teachings of Jesus are according to the Covenant in "The Valediction of Moses", and "The Moses Scroll" by Ross Nichols. Because the Covenant has no such rule (blasphemy of the Holy Spirit), it is questionable that Jesus was adding an unforgivable sin to what Elohim said. God said who is cursed. God said who is blessed. It's that simple, and we should no need to rely on a Pope, Priest or an Orthodox Rabbi to understand God. It is by his teachings in Matthew that Jesus is evidently proven to be "that prophet" spoken of by Moses in Deuteronomy 18, as anyone should also be able to see that Jesus (Joshua/Y'shua) was teaching us to repent to serve God and keep His Covenant as given. He was renewing the Covenant to mankind and Israel, and his hope was that at some future time they would again say: "Blessed is he who comes in the name of Elohim. Get yourself a copy of either "THE VALEDICTION OF MOSES" or "THE MOSES SCROLL" and note that at the end of the Curses, Elohim stated that a future generation would be aware of what He said that day, and that He knew of "the schemes" they would devise. (altering the Covenant and the various oral torahs and Zohar, etc?)

Since Jesus was teaching what God and the prophets had told, it was surely unjust and to their own demise that they rejected, falsely condemned, and crucified Jesus. God raised him from the dead, and the disciples testified he ascended to heaven, as foretold by Daniel, to "sit on the throne on the right hand of the Power on High." One of the "Watergate" convicted converted to Christianity, and his reason was there was no way that 11 men all died, quite apart from each other, for simply refusing to say Jesus did not raise from the dead. He knew from personal experience that the few involved in Watergate could never have done likewise. He was absolutely convinced by this one fact that they had to have been telling the truth, and of their conviction to this being true because they paid for their testimony of fact with their lives. As Psalm 110:1 says, "The LORD (Elohim/YHWH) sayeth unto my lord: Sit thou at My right hand until I make thine enemies thy footstool." Elohim has been faithful to His word, and so will continue to remain faithful to it - but not to those who dared alter His Covenant, and then teach not living as He had told them to live, but instead filter the Scripture through musings of wayward self-deluded and self-aggrandizing Rabbi, whom Moses, Isaiah, Ezekiel, Daniel, Jeremiah, Micah, Isaiah and Zechariah would surely have warned us to ignore. (See who God said to hear: Deut. 4, 12, 13, 18)) Had Orthodox Judaism been teaching and living as Elohim decreed, they would have a long history of testifying to the nations of the great wisdom and source of blessings they (and we) had received from Elohim in the Covenant. Had they done the will of God, Jerusalem would be world renown for it's justice, righteousness, and pleading the case of the needy and defenseless widows and orphans. What we see today of her willful injustice and bigotry is the exact opposite of what Elohim said they are to do! "Israel" the "nation" has nothing to do with Abraham, who even pleaded on behalf of wicked cities that ended up being destroyed by fire and brimstone. There is no righteousness in Isreal – but it is exactly as Elohim declared they would become – worse and worse, lower and lower, they are despised among all the nations for their corrupting those who serve them alone. (Epstien child trafficking, Musad, World Bank, Federal Reserve, and the dual citizens who run Agencies in the US to the hurt of the whole earth and mankind. They have also taken over all the mainstream news networks, starting with the printing press telling the lies that lead up to WWI, WWII, and even Disney today promoting evils to our youth.

Proof of Orthodox Judaism defying the Covenant is easily seen in this fact: The Sabbath Instruction from Elohim is very short and direct. The "Oral Torah" instruction on how to keep the Sabbath is over 500 pages long. God said nothing was too hard to understand or to do, but according to the Rabbi, you must keep their rules to be faithful – which is a direct lie against Elohim Almighty, and against their fellows, and against all mankind, because they did not abide in the sure words given by Elohim. Other things they demand of their followers is ceremonial hand washing – where no such thing was given by Elohim. In fact, none of the Covenant is about ceremonies, but all of it directly relates to just and equitable living amongst those God calls "My people," which was to be seen by others as just and good, and thereby draw others to Elohim and the "good paths" given for us to live by. It is very hard to not smirk at the sight of all the Rabbi with their black clothes and funny hats dancing around when they celebrate or pretend copulation when they pray at the "wailing wall" of the Roman fortress foundation in Jerusalem. The Temple has been gone for almost 2000 years. Didn't Josephus say the Temple was totally razed? (including the foundation)

Christians have been stumbling around teaching Paul, but where is the record that Judaism has been famous to be faithful to Elohim and being the shining beacon of hope and trust and faithfulness to Elohim, the one true God of Abraham, Isaac and Jacob???? Adding false charges against Jesus is not going to validate their first charges made against him. Their charges can be proven to be lies against Jesus and God then, as they can also be proven so today - if our judgment is based on the Covenant Standards given by God at Sinai! See "V" - all have been led away from the Standard given by Elohim! Let's get back on track and observe the "Covenant", and "the blessings and the curses," as they also find harmony with the teachings of Joshua (Jesus) in Matthew, when we have the courage to realize "our" accounts were altered, starting in the First Century (about 85 CE). Carefully note how these fit to the Ten Commandments account in "V". One can also observe the charges against Israel by the Prophets were much more in keeping to "V" than our current Bibles tell us.

"Blessed is the man who has Elohim as his god, and who prostrates himself only to him, and who serves him alone."

"Blessed is the man who sanctifies the seventh day and rests on it."

"Blessed is he who honors his father and his mother."

"Blessed is the man who does not avenge or exact retribution for the soul of his brother."

"Blessed is the man who does not defile the wife of his fellow."

"Blessed is the man who does not cheat his fellow."

"Blessed is the man who does not swear in my name falsely."

"Blessed is the man who does not deceive or lie to his fellow."

"Blessed is he who does not lust after anyone belonging to his fellow."

"Blessed is the man who loves his fellow."

"Blessed is the man who upholds all the proclamations of this teaching to perform them."

"See if you truly heed the voice of your god, taking care to do all his commandments, then all of these blessings will befall you: Blessed are you in the city, blessed are you in the fields, blessed are your firstling and your remnant. Blessed are the fruit of your loins and the fruit of your land, and the wombs of your cattle and the bellies of your sheep. Blessed are you in your coming, and blessed are you in your going. Elohim will set your enemies - defeated- before you. Elohim will order blessing upon all your handwork. Elohim will establish you as a holy people; all the peoples of the land will behold and fear you. Elohim will open the heavens for you, to give rain for your land in its season. You will lend to many nations, you will not borrow. You will be only on top, you will not be on bottom. Elohim will make you abound only in goodness upon the good land that Elohim, god of your fathers, is giving you."

Pay very close attention to the decrees of Elohim. If He is true to His word, it should be easily seen Israel has not been faithful to Him for a long, long time, and current efforts by Zionist Orthodox Judaism will likely meet the most harsh judgment from Elohim as has ever been meted out on the earth!! *If God said they would become a byword amongst the nations - I would suspect He is the One who caused these things, because that is what He said He would do, so why do they blame Jesus and his disciples????? Why not blame God for doing as He said He would? By claiming Jesus did this, do they believe Jesus is God?*

"Cursed is the man who does a carving or a casting, the handiwork of a craftsman."

"Cursed is the man who does work on the seventh day."

"Cursed is he who disgraces his father and mother."

"Cursed is he who strikes down his fellow in secret."

"Cursed is the man who approaches any of his kin, or who commits adultery with the wife of his fellow, or who copulates with any animal."

"Cursed is he who moves the boundary marker of his fellow."

"Cursed is the man who swears falsely in my name."

"Cursed is he who takes a bribe to give false judgment against his comrade."

"Cursed is the man who desires and lusts after the wife of his fellow, his daughter, his female slave, or anything that is his."

"Cursed is the man who hates his brother in his heart."

"Cursed is the man who does not uphold all the proclamations of this teaching to perform them."

"If you do not heed the voice of Elohim, taking care to do all his commandments and decrees, then all of these curses will befall you: Cursed are you in the city, cursed are you in the field, cursed are your firstling and your remnant. Cursed are the fruit of your loins and the fruit of your land, the wombs of your cattle and the bellies of your sheep. Cursed are you in your coming, and cursed are you in your going. Elohim will set you - defeated- before your enemies. Elohim will cast the execration upon all your handiwork. Elohim will make you an epitaph, a proverb, and a saying among all the nations of the land. Elohim will stop up the heavens. The stranger settled in your midst will rise higher and higher; you will descend lower and lower. He will lend to you; you will not lend to him. Elohimn will demolish and eradicate you from the land that you are going into to possess....."<u>Be strong and resolute, do not fear and do not panic. For Elohim, your god - he is the one who walks alongside you. He will not let go of you, he will not abandon you. Now write down this teaching, so that this teaching may be a witness before you, since it will not be forgotten from the mouths of your descendants, for I know the schemes that you devise.</u>" These are the words that Moses instructed all the children of Israel according to the order of YHWH on the plains of Moab before his death.

It sure seems to me that Elohim knew what I'm bringing up today would certainly happen in the course of the history of Israel, and the history of mankind upon the earth. Those are the words Elohim gave to Moses – not the "Oral Torah's" of Orthodox Judaism and

Zionists who have defied every Standard given by Elohim to then proclaim: "I did it my way." Learn some lessons from history – who invented Communism, as it defies every Commandment given by Elohim.

Malichi 3:16 - 18, Dead Sea Scrolls Bible:

"Then those who feared the LORD spoke one to another, and the LORD listened, and heard, and <u>a book of remembrance was written before him</u>, for those who feared the LORD, and that thought upon his name. So that they shall be mine, says the LORD of hosts, even my own possession, <u>in the day that I make; and I will spare them, as a man spares his own son that serves him. Then you will again distinguish between the righteous and the wicked, between the one who serves God and the one who serves him not</u>."

We must use the unaltered words of Elohim to know these things. Believing those who lie against God will be like following the blind leaders into the ditch. It is no wonder that "Christianity" is now divided across 20,000 different sects. Our unity must be based upon that which Elohim Himself said "My people" will use for their Standard.

1917 Jewish Publication Society, Psalm 2:

<u>1</u>Why are the nations in an uproar?

And why do the peoples mutter in vain?

<u>2</u>The kings of the earth stand up,

And the rulers take counsel together,

Against the LORD, and against His anointed:

<u>3</u>'Let us break their bands asunder,

And cast away their cords from us.'

<u>4</u>He that sitteth in heaven laugheth,

The Lord hath them in derision.

<u>5</u>Then will He speak unto them in His wrath,

And affright them in His sore displeasure:

<u>6</u>'Truly it is I that have established My king

Upon Zion, My holy mountain.'

7I will tell of the decree:

The LORD said unto me: 'Thou art My son,

This day have I begotten thee. ((Quote of the voice from heaven at Jesus' baptism?))

8Ask of Me, and I will give the nations for thine inheritance,

And the ends of the earth for thy possession.

9Thou shalt break them with a rod of iron;

Thou shalt dash them in pieces like a potter's vessel.'

10*Now therefore, O ye kings, be wise;*

Be admonished, ye judges of the earth.

11*Serve the LORD (Elohim/YHWH) with fear,*

And rejoice with trembling.

12*Do homage in purity, lest He be angry, and ye perish in the way,*

When suddenly His wrath is kindled.

Happy are all they that take refuge in Him."

[[[Does not say "kiss the son" as Christian Bibles do. (broad implications to Christian beliefs and doctrines).]]]

Jesus taught to serve Elohim alone. Jesus (Joshua) never taught to worship or pray to himself, but to repent and pray to do the will of Elohim faithfully, as Elohim decreed, not as the Pharisees and Sages demanded of the Jews of his day, or what has further developed via many "Oral Torah" requirements in Orthodox Judaism. Proof Jesus was teaching the Covenant is the "greatest commandment" was the first, and the last of the blessings is to be compared and conjoined to it – loving Elohim first, and loving our fellow as ourselves. To keep the Covenant requires our love for God to be reflected in our love and care for our fellow mankind (because man was made in the image of God).

What I am sharing here proves much of the New Testament are fabrications that have led millions away from the provable Truth - Truth being defined as the Proclamations and Instructions of God in the Torah, Psalms and Prophets. God said the "Ten Declarations" are the Covenant, and the Covenant tablets of stone were placed in the Ark of the Covenant, and the Mercy Seat was the lid of the Ark of the Covenant that both protected the tablets and symbolized the Mercy Seat: that the Mercy of God covers those who keep the Covenant as He had written it.

If there were angels facing the Ark from either end, this signifies that Elohim gives His angels charge to look over those who are faithful to the Covenant Truth and Mercy of Elohim. The oldest account of the Pact/Covenant was published in 2021. "The Valediction of Moses" may be the most important book published in 3000 years! It was amazing to see the ancient Covenant Standards accord to the teachings of Jesus in Matthew! I now believe Jesus was killed for daring to tell people the true Covenant Standards (Proclamations/Blessings/Curses) via his teachings, which shows they were Elohim inspired via the Spirit Jesus received at his baptism by John the Baptist. Although altered 1000 years before Jesus, his teachings match the Covenant Standards seen from the days of Ezekiel! Jesus made no claim to be God or co-creator; one cannot be a "son of man" and Elohim at the same time.

Who is the enemy of mankind but those who have perverted the Teachings of God and have killed those who tried to speak up about what God really said? It started with Satan, the Serpent in Eden, and it has continued through Orthodox Judaisms' despotic leadership (see the charges against Judaism leadership as found in the major prophets - this is what they said, and what Jesus said; I'm merely pointing this Scriptural point out). The Catholic Church has like fruits, to kill those who dared speak up to try to warn people the Church was evil and lying - such is the early history of Christianity. I have little doubt Paul was a plant of Rome, via corrupted Judaistic Pharisee leadership, sent and fostered to obliterate the REAL truth of Elohim to mankind. Anyone with eyes to see, anyone with ears to hear - look at 2 Timothy 4 and see that Paul himself was defeated in a trial that took place (Revelation 2?) and that EVERYONE abandoned him thereafter!!! Paul stood out as a rejected liar against God and Jesus by the First Century Church!!! Citing Paul's writings in any way was only resurrected by the Roman Church, those who resurrected his lies against God and Jesus, and who also denounced anyone who dared speak the truth of God to be a "Heretic!" Believe it or not, my own brother, a Church of Christ preacher, called me a "heretic" for not believing the lies of Paul – Jesus was a the literal "Son of God" *per Paul's teachings), that Jesus was a "sacrifice for sin" (per the teachings of Paul that cast the blessed Teachings of God aside to facilitate his lies), or to dare realize Paul was not one of the apostles of Jesus. So it is when you dare speak the truth – your own families may become your enemies – just as Jesus foretold in Matthew!

The time has come to awaken or to perish. The choice is yours to make for yourself, but Elohim said to "Choose life, that ye may live!"

God warned us, Jesus warned the Jews, and we have inherited lies from our "fathers" of faith. Unless you repent of lies against God, you are effectively siding with Satan and those who seek to destroy mankind from the face of the earth. Paul was nothing but a liar, and for all his flowery remarks, he taught doing the opposite of what God, the Prophets and Jesus taught! Mark, Luke and John all testify against the Original Jesus. Paul hated God so much that he said the Covenant (Law) was not given by Elohim, but came as a curse via lowly angels. So, if you hate God, choose to believe the lies of Paul and Satan, but know Elohim said He will be true to His unaltered words of life and death – blessed – versus - cursed.

Cease evil and learn to do good; do no evil - this must begin by renewing your mind through repenting to live by the words God and Jesus spoke - not Paul or other "New Testament" books beyond Matthew, and even Matthew was obviously altered. Wake up!!

What sane and reasonable person cannot recognize the Teachings of Elohim and Jesus (Joshua) are for our good? Can you consider a world where you have no fear of your property being stolen, or a world where you have no fear of someone lying, injuring, murdering or plotting against you to take what you have, or defame your character? If we all desire to live together in peace, how can we support the murder of the innocent, the theft of property or a good name - let alone believe the lies of those who only stir up mire and muddy the waters of life and good will amongst mankind!? Can we imagine a world where people don't lie about others, but only truth and justice prevail? How much evil would be prevented if those who falsely charge another were to be guilty of the crimes they accused the other person of doing? (This is in the "Law" as given by Elohim, but Judaism has been king of false accusations since they got away with it in having Jesus killed, only to be compounded by declaring themselves blessed and justified for having done so!)

Protection of the innocent from attacks at all levels would certainly have a great impact on everyone. If we all paid attention to the Teachings of God, it is likely that even gossiping would be a thing of the past! Those simple Teachings and Commandments of God, 10 just, perfectly reasonable and doable Teachings, when understood by the breadth and depth given to them by God and the Prophets of the Holy Scripture would likely put most religious institutions out of business unless they abandon telling lies about God and His Instructions in Righteousness, Justice and Mercy. And what of those who had to steal a loaf of bread to survive? The Commandment, as given, was not to steal the wealth of another – and who can honestly say stealing a loaf of bread is to be worthily punished by making them a slave – to then steal their God given life and life's work for yourself? Such a thought was justified at one time. See the writings of Michael Hoffman about the history of white slavery. This is the root of the meaning of "kidnapping." In his writings one can also observe that usery (lending money at interest) was considered a capital crime until the Roman Church partnered in banking interests with some wealthy Jews of historical fame. The Covenant Decrees are not a "living document" to be re interpreted by each generation, the Covenant as given by Elohim was to be taught to each successive generation – and it has not been so taught for 3000 years or so. Hear the matter out – see if it doesn't make sense. The Covenant is not a "living document", but a Covenant to live by, and thereby be blessed by Elohim.

Upon close observation, there is no commandment that is too hard to understand or do. Why have Christians believed the reports of Paul that the "Law" was too hard to keep, and that no one can be "saved" who seeks to do the will of God as He gave it in the Everlasting Covenant ratified at Sinai? If we set His Standards aside, what is to become of us as individuals or a society at large? Look around today and observe how much evil is multiplying because of "lawlessness" as defined by God. Are we to believe it is now OK to lie, because some Rabbi twirled a chicken, or we believe Jesus died for our sins, as the "once for all" sacrifice for sin? (the big lie) – that we are incapable or excused from doing what is right in the eyes of God and fellow humans? How can this be true if the only record from Jesus' disciples has no such account in it? Who, then, told us so? The idea is conveyed no where in all the unaltered Law or Prophets or Psalms or the gospel account written by the disciples of Joshua (Jesus)!

Is it now justifiable to lie against God and say what He has spoken is ineffective to accomplish what He said His Teachings are able to accomplish in anyone who will observe His Covenant to live just and reasonable lives – to live according to His Covenant? To observe His Covenant to do them? Which one of the Ten Teachings is unreasonable? Which is too hard to do? Really - can anyone prove they are impossible? or unreasonable? or unjust? or given as a curse?!!! Such thoughts are demon inspired lies against Elohim and His anointed one.

Which was Paul incapable to do, that he said he was not able to keep the Teachings of God given through Moses, which was the fulfillment of the promise to Abraham to bless those of all nations through his offspring? There is no other record of history that God has revealed Himself and the Standards (conditions He gave in the Covenant) that show they are from Him and are certainly able to accomplish that for which He gave them. There are no "spiritual mysteries" involved, and those Teachings of God remain true to this day, but few study them to see how beautiful they really are, or that they inter-relate to also provide us the wisdom needed to know the difference between those who serve God and those who say they do, but are His enemies and in rebellion against Him and His anointed one.

As Jesus taught: "By their fruits ye shall know them." The "fruits" are living by His Covenant, those are the "fruits God is due" from those who serve Him as the One True God. Worship of God is doing the 10 Decrees. He called Israel and the multitude out of Egypt to serve Him, which is what the Covenant is.

The "Covenant," according to God and Moses, is the Ten Decrees and the "blessings and the curses", not the "613 Commandments" invented by a Jewish Rabbi in the 1200's, nor is there any truth of God to be found in the Rabbinical Decree of the "Seven Noahite Laws." Both of these defy what God and Moses said.

Jesus understood what God was saying, and through his teachings in Matthew we can, should, and must observe the context of every Teaching of Jesus is the Everlasting Covenant of God, as ratified between God and all who choose life, of all nations, not just Jews, as they pretend. The narrative of the Hebrew Scripture proves the "multitude of nations" ratified the Covenant when given, and were also present when the Covenant was "renewed" upon entry into the Land. Judaism abandoned God and were following Rabbi's and Sages of the Ages. Proof of this existing to this day can be observed in their current understanding of their history to begin with the "rabbinical age" about 300 BC, rather than when God ratified the Covenant at Sinai. Jesus (Joshua 2) was also renewing the Covenant is for men of all nations who choose to serve the God of Abraham, Isaac and Jacob.

Even though the World Bank and FED, who trade our birth certificate as a commodity, and thereby claim to possess our soul, and that you are nothing but a "monster" (Per Jordon Maxwell in discussion of symbolism, the FED, and Maratime Law), that piece of paper is not your soul, no matter what they think. What if some think they can loan money to others without interest, based on the Teachings of God in the Torah, but they are establishing the money upon the value of pretending to sell the souls of the Gentiles on the open market (note birth certificates have a red serial number and the name is all capital letters (Corporation), and then take the money generated falsely on presumed possession of others souls: how is that different than considering them to be a slave to be possessed, traded and sold? – it's just hidden. All souls belong to God, not the FED or World Bank. This really isn't about that, but I'd be remiss to not say anything about it. (See "The Secret Relationship Between Blacks and Jews" volume 1, and "Planet Rothschild" by M.S.King; I believe the interviews with Jordan Maxwell have been deleted from the internet by the thought police.)

YHWH declared the souls of all men are His possession – not the possession of liars and satans. Do you desire to be freed from the prison houses of lies, to then serve the One True God, and experience all that He offers you? Learn from God. Pay close attention to His Instruction that you *become wise and abandon lies against Him*. One of the main purposes of the founders of the United States of America goes back to the founders from the Colonies – that of religious freedom – to be able to choose to serve God according to your own conscience, not by the Decree of the "Church State" as it existed from Rome to England. If we have been free to worship God, why seek to be in submission to those who falsely accused Jesus, and then had Rome participate with them in his execution??? (The "Orthodox Judaism Rabbi who evolved to have codified their "oral torah" as superior to the Everlasting Covenant of Elohim. Consider how long they have fostered the altered Covenant (3000 years?).

To know "the" truth requires understanding of foundations, as religious builders abandoned the foundations about 2000 years ago, but the plans still exist, so long as we are willing to revisit the Teachings of God and Jesus from the most original records and ignore the dirt piled upon them by those who chose to defy God and His Instructions – study will require use of both the Hebrew Scripture and the Dead Sea Scrolls Bible, because both Christians and Jews have altered their respective accounts. The task is to dig down through the dirt to build our lives on the Rock foundation of the Teachings of Elohim and the Elohim inspired teachings of Jesus (account in Matthew that he was begotten of Elohim at his baptism),

The Matthew account of the temptation of Jesus in the wilderness establishes core principles for an orderly foundation to build one's life on obedience to God through understanding and living as God Instructed. I was also misled about that account, as though it was only given to show Jesus was "tempted in like matter with all things that are common to the temptations of all mankind." Rather than being about "temptations," the account was given to provide guidance when approaching the Scripture, and to not pit the words or blessings of God against Himself, or ourselves, that we are to seek the pathway He gave to "know the truth" and for it to be our light for our pathway in life. The salvation and blessing of God is based on living by the reasonable, reliable, and just standards given by God. God is the Teacher and Redeemer; there is no other (Isaiah 43). Jesus made no claim to be God incarnate, and we can know this because the record of his chosen disciples (Matthew) tells of no such thing, especially noting the Hebrew Matthew account before it was altered in the Greek account to make it appear less contradictory to the additional gospel accounts of Mark, Luke and John. We are far better off to observe the depths of Matthew than to muse against it. Matthew may well prove the other gospels are not worthy of study or belief. Matthew may also prove the rest of the New Testament is nonsense and the source of divisions between those who believe in God and Jesus! Have we all inherited lies from our fathers? Do we love Truth enough to believe God and abandon those who try to tell us lies against Him? (*2 Corinthians 3: 6-17) The Prophets in the Hebrew Scripture gave much clarity to basic principles, but the Teachings of Jesus were given for those of all nations and have more breadth and depth than anyone since Moses. Perhaps the greatest thing we can gain from Jesus' teachings is the proper and blessed relationship between a man and his Maker, which requires proper relationship between himself and other men to be a reflection of his relationship to the One True God. Did God, who made man in His image, who said upon man being placed upon the earth to be "very good", would mankind need to rule and subdue the earth with truth, justice, and mercy? This is the basic core message of the Ten Commandments. Is this why Jesus placed the "Greatest Commandment" (Thou shalt love the Lord they God, and Him only thou shalt serve) as indivisible from "love your neighbor as yourself" to be "like unto the first Commandment"? Jesus was showing us that the first commandment cannot be separated from the blessings and the curses, because loving our fellow is the last of the Blessings, and "hating your fellow in your heart" is violation of the 10th commandment that was deleted by unfaithful priests in the days near Ezekiel. While Matthew 19:6 discusses marriage, the first principle teaching about not dividing what God has joined together is the "Ten Decrees" given by God and ratified by all present at Mount Sinai. The Teachings in those Decrees of God were given that we might choose life and live! And they are the most misrepresented words of God in all the Christian "Bibles" that have ever been printed and read by millions of people! They are also the most misrepresented words in all the Orthodox Judaism Talmud or writings of their "Sages of the Ages." Let's all stop the nonsense and face the same words of God as He joined them all together into the "Everlasting Covenant." (Psalm 119) It is still a false claim to say Jesus taught against the Covenant Law of God, and Matthew proves the context of all his teachings is the Covenant, as given by God.

"(2 Corintians 3: 6-17: (6) Who also hath made us able ministers of the new testament; not of the letter, but of the spirit: for *the letter killeth*, **but the spirit giveth life. (7) But if** *the ministration of death*, **written and** *engraven in stones*, **was glorious, so that the children of Israel could not stedfastly behold the face of Moses for** the glory of his countenance; which glory *was to be done away*: (8) How shall not the ministration of the spirit be rather glorious? (9) For if *the ministration of condemnation* be glory, much more doth the ministration of righteousness exceed in glory. (10) For even that which was made glorious had no glory in this respect, by reason of the glory that excelleth. (11) For if that which is *done away* was glorious, much more that which remaineth is glorious. (12) Seeing then that we have such hope, we use great plainness of speech: (13) And not as Moses, which put a vail over his face, that the children of Israel could not stedfastly look to the end of that which is abolished: (14) But *their minds were blinded*: for until this day remaineth the same vail untaken away in the *reading of the old testament*; which vail is *done away in Christ*. (15) But even unto this day, *when Moses is read, the vail is upon their heart*. (16) Nevertheless when it shall turn to the Lord, *the vail shall be taken away*. (17) Now the Lord is that Spirit: and where the Spirit of the Lord is, there is *liberty*. (ASV)"(one famous lie of Saul)

The record of Matthew will prove the other gospels to be what they are. When alterations are found they expose errors, both great and small, and we should never fear to trust the Teachings God gave to know and live by. God gave His Teachings to elevate us - not to curse or condemn us. Yes, there is the matter of the blessings and the curses - and it relates solely upon who will accept His Instructions to do them by making them the Standard to live by - as opposed to those who will not honor the Words of God in the Everlasting Covenant. The matter, according to God, is who will make His instruction to be their standard of life and faith - God given Decrees to live by. God is the one who promised blessing and kindness towards those who observe His word, and He is also the one who said those who reject His Instruction are cursed.

Exodus 20: 1-7; "**God spoke all these statements, saying: "I the LORD am your God who brought you out of the land of Egypt, from the house of bondage: You shall have no other gods besides Me. You shall not make yourself a sculptured image nor any likeness of that which is in the heavens above, or on the earth below or in the water beneath the earth. You shall not bow down to them or serve them. For I the LORD your God am an impassioned God, visiting the guilt of the parents upon the children, upon the third and upon the fourth generations, <u>of those that reject Me</u>; but <u>showing kindness to the thousandth generation to those who love Me and keep My commandments</u>. You shall not swear falsely by the name of the LORD your God; for the LORD will not clear one who swears falsely by His name.**"(*from ETZ HAYIM edition of the Torah*)

Exodus 20: 1-7: Stone Edition by Artscroll; **"God spoke all these statements, saying:** "I am HASHEM, your God, Who has taken you out of the land of Egypt, from the house of slavery. You shall not recognize the gods of others in My presence. You shall not make yourself a carved image nor any likeness of that which is in the heavens above or on the earth below or in the water beneath the earth. You shall not prostrate yourself to them nor worship them, for I am HASHEM, your God - a jealous God, Who visits the sin of fathers upon children to the third and fourth generations, <u>for My enemies</u>; but <u>Who shows kindness for thousands (of generations) to those who love Me and observe My commandments</u>. You shall not take the Name of HASHEM, your God, in vain, for HASHEM will not absolve anyone who takes His Name in vain."

***Note a slight variation between the two translations - Stone Edition: "for my enemies;" and "of those that reject Me" in ETZ HYIM. Since both are using the same Hebrew Text - it seems safe to understand that those who reject the Instruction and Covenant of God are those who are His enemies? **Carefully note the differences between what we have compared to "V."**

"Valediction of Moses" account: (1)"I am Elohim, your god, who freed you from the land of Egypt, from the slave-house. (2) You shall not have any other gods. You shall not make a carving or any image that is in the heavens above or the earth below or in the waters beneath the earth. You shall not prostrate yourselves before them, and you shall not serve them. I am Elohim, your god."

Ia mankind incapable to repent of lies against Elohim and His anointed one? (Psalm 2)

God repeatedly gave simple instructions. His Teachings are not too hard to understand, or too hard to do. This is what God said in **Deuteronomy 30: 11-20**. The fact is that God said it is no "mystery" at all. Read the word of God and know the truth that will set you free to serve the One True God and see if He doesn't bless you as He said He will.

"For this commandment I give you today is not too difficult for you or beyond your reach. It is not in heaven, that you would need to ask, "Who will ascend into heaven to get it for us and proclaim it, that we may obey it?" And it is not beyond the sea, that you would need to ask, "Who will cross the sea to get it for us and proclaim it, that we may obey it?" But the word is very near you, in your mouth and in your heart, so that you may obey it. See, I have set before you today life and prosperity, as well as death and disaster. For I am commanding you today to love Elohim your God, to walk in His ways, and to keep His commandments, statutes, and ordinances, so that you may live and increase, and Elohim your God may bless you in the land you are entering to possess. But if your heart turns away and you do not listen, but are drawn away to bow down

to other gods and worship them, I declare to you today that you will surely perish; you shall not prolong your days in the land you are crossing the Jordan to possess. I call heaven and earth as witnesses against you today that I have set before you life and death, blessing and cursing. So choose life, so that you and your descendants may live, and that you may love Elohim your God, obey Him, and hold fast to Him. For He is your life, and He will prolong your life in the land Elohim swore to give to your fathers, Abraham, Isaac, and Jacob."

God never expected or demanded perfection as told by Paul in: "For all have sinned and fallen short of the glory of God." Throughout the Torah we are told of His abundant forgiveness and kindness towards those who wholeheartedly repent to do His will – to abandon evil and learn to do good. This is the message of Isaiah 1, where God said: "Come, let us reason together"! The message of Elohim has been consistent from the beginning of the Hebrew Scriptures, but men have altered His words of life!

What kind of God will not forgive anyone unless He had His only Son slain as a sacrifice so He could see the blood of His Son covering the persons who are His enemies to see them as part (or extension) of His Son? This may be a frightful thought for many Christians to consider but let's do a reality check to see if that belief has any foundation in the Teachings, Decrees or Justice as given by Elohim, or if it was taught as a foundational principle by Jesus in Matthew.

What reasonable and sane person would not be willing to forgive someone unless they killed their own son to forgive someone who had wronged them? Wouldn't this be nonsense, and dare we say evil?! Is Elohim unable to forgive without taking life?! We need to face the fact that the book of "Hebrews" testifies against Elohim, the Covenant, and even the mercy and goodness of God.

Isaiah chapter one proves that living uprightly by His Teachings about justice and righteousness must precede our worship or sacrifice to Him, or our prayers for His blessing our lives, or requests to Him in prayer. The truth is plainly told through the prophet Ezekiel in chapter eighteen, which says nothing about blood sacrifice being required by God to forgive, but that repenting and faithfulness to doing what He said is good is required. It always has been! I have found no word of God that foretells killing Himself or His direct offspring so He will forgive His enemies of their sins against Him! Neither did Jesus indicate any such reason for why he was to be crucified! No, in Matthew the reason he was unjustly put to death was to fulfill prophecy in Scripture - not to provide blood atonement to the enemies of God.

As for the account of God commanding Abraham about Isaac: God stayed Abraham's hand because He did not desire human sacrifice ; it was one of the tests God put Abraham through to see if he would be faithful and obedient, not a foreshadowing to prove Jesus' shed blood on the cross was the slain "lamb of God." After having read some in the Hebrew account translated into English, it could be the passage was mistranslated and that God called for Abraham to take Isaac to the mountain to make a sacrificial offering to God, not to offer Isaac as a sacrifice to God. The viewpoint I share certainly fits with the statement of God to Israel regarding the practice of child sacrifice to Moloch or Baal: God said when corrupted Israel did this that such a thing had never entered His mind and that it was an abomination! Think about this and see if you can disprove it by the unaltered Hebrew Scripture account. (Dead Sea Scrolls Bible and the Hebrew Scripture)

Let's review what God says in Isaiah chapter one, and in Ezekiel chapter eighteen:

Isaiah 1:

The vision of Isaiah son of Amoz, which he saw concerning Judah and Jerusalem, in the days of Uzziah, Jotham, Ahaz, and Hezekiah, kings of Judah: Hear, O heavens, and give ear, O earth, for Elohim has spoken: "Children have I raised and exalted, but they have rebelled against Me. An ox knows his owner, and a donkey his master's trough; but Israel does not know, My people does not comprehend."

Woe! (They are) a sinful nation, a people weighed down by iniquity, evil offspring, destructive children! They have forsaken Elohim; they have angered the Holy One of Israel, and have turned their back (to Him). For what have you been smitten, since you continue to act perversely? Each head (is smitten) with sickness; each heart (with) infirmity. From the sole of the foot to the head, nothing in him is whole; (only) injury, bruise, and festering wound: They have not been treated and they have not been bandaged, and (the wound) has not been softened with oil. Your country is desolate; your cities are burned with fire; as for your land - strangers consume its (yield) in your presence; it is desolate as if overturned by foreigners. The daughter of Zion is left like a booth in a vineyard, like a shed in a field of gourds, like a city besieged. Had not Elohim, Master of Legions, left us a trace of a remnant, we would have been like Sodom; we would have resembled Gomorrah!

Hear the word of Elohim, O chiefs of Sodom, give ear to the teaching of our God, O people of Gomorrah:

Why do I need your numerous sacrifices? Says Elohim. I am sated with elevation-offerings of rams and the fat of fatlings; the blood of bulls, sheep and goats I do not desire. When you come to appear before Me, who sought this from your hand, to trample My Courtyards? Bring your worthless meal-offering no longer; it is incense of abomination to Me. (As for) the New Moon and Sabbath, and your

calling of convocations, I cannot abide your appointed times; they have become a burden upon Me; I am weary of bearing (them). When you spread your hands (in prayer), I will hide My eyes from you; even if you were to intensify your prayer, I will not listen; your hands are replete with blood. <u>Wash yourselves, purify yourselves, remove the evil of your deeds from before My eyes; cease doing evil. Learn to do good, seek justice, vindicate the victim, render justice to the orphan, take up the grievance of the widow."</u> (Note how this fits with the "great commission of Matthew and the sermon of Peter on Pentecost: hear, believe, repent, be baptized, grow in the will of God as taught by Jesus – to keep whatsoever his disciples said he had first taught them, which certainly taught the proper interpretation and application of the Law.)

<u>**Come, now, let us reason together, says Elohim. If your sins are like scarlet they will become white as snow; if they have become red as crimson, they will become (white) as wool. If you are willing and obey, you will eat the goodness of the land. But if you refuse and rebel, you will be devoured by the sword - for the mouth of Elohim has spoken.**</u>

How the faithful city has become a harlot! - she had been full of justice, righteousness lodged in her, but now murderers! Your silver has become dross, your heady wine diluted with water. Your princes are rebellious and associates of thieves; each of them loves bribery and pursues payments. They do not render justice to the orphan; the grievance of the widow does not come to them.

Therefore - the word of the Lord, Elohim, Master of Legions, Mighty One of Israel: Oh, <u>I shall be relieved of My adversaries, and I shall avenge Myself of My enemies! I will turn My hand against you, until I refine your dross as with lye and I remove all your base metal. Then I will restore your judges as at first, and your counselors as at the beginning; after that you will be called "City of Righteousness, Faithful City." Zion will be redeemed through justice, and those who return to her through righteousness; but calamity (awaits) rebels and sinners together, and those who forsake Elohim will perish</u>; for they will become ashamed of the idolatrous elms that you desired, and you will be embarrassed over the gardens that you chose. For you will be like an elm tree with withered leaves, and like a garden without water. The mighty will be like flax and its maker like a spark; and the two of them will burn together, with no one to extinguish it."

(SE - "HASHEM" replaced with Elohim as "HASHEM" means "The NAME"

(Note that proper living precedes acceptable worship - God desires our living justly and righteously - not blood sacrifices. Also recall who God said are unjust or cursed in the Decrees and the blessings and the curses. **Most important to the "Christian" beliefs** from Paul - God does not absolve those who are His enemies - even if they are Israel!)

Ezekiel 18:

"The word of Elohim came to me, saying:

Why do you relate this parable upon the land of Israel, saying, 'The fathers eat sour grapes, but the teeth of the sons are set on edge!' As I live - the word of the Lord YHWH/ELOHIM - (I swear) that there will no longer be anyone among you who uses this parable in Israel. Behold, all souls are Mine; like the soul of the father, so the soul of the son, they are Mine. The soul that sins - it shall die.

<u>If a man is righteous and practices justice and righteousness; he does not partake of idolatrous sacrifices upon the mountains</u> (or twirl chickens?); **does not lift his eyes towards the idols of the House of Israel; does not defile his neighbor's wife nor approach an impure woman; does not oppress any man; returns collateral for a debt; does not rob any loot; gives his bread to the hungry and covers the naked with clothing; does not give loans with usury nor take interest; withholds his hand from corruption; executes true justice between man and man; goes according to My decrees and observes My ordinances to practice truth - he is a righteous man; he shall surely live - the word of the Lord, YHWH/ELOHIM.**

If he begets a violent son, who sheds blood, who does any of these sins to his brother, who does not do all these good deeds: for he even partakes of idolatrous sacrifices upon the mountains; defiles his neighbor's wife; oppresses the poor and the needy; robs loot; does not return collateral; lifts his eyes towards the idols; commits abomination; gives loans with usury and takes interest - should he live? He shall not live! He has committed all these abominations; he shall surely die and his blood will be upon himself.

Then if he begets a son who sees all the sins of his father that he had done; he sees, but does not do (acts) like them;: He does not partake of idolatrous sacrifices upon the mountains; does not lift his eyes towards the idols of the House of Israel; does not defile his neighbor's wife; does not oppress any man; does not keep collateral, does not rob any loot; gives his bread to the hungry and covers the naked with clothing; withholds his hand from harming the poor; does not take usury or interest; obeys My ordinance and follows My decrees - he shall not doe for his father's iniquity; he shall surely live.

His father, because he has cruelly oppressed others, has robbed loot from his brother and did that which is not good among his people - behold, he died for his sin. Yet you say, 'Why did the son not bear the iniquity of the father?' But the son performed justice and righteousness, and observed all My decrees and performed them; he should surely live! The soul that sins it shall die! A son shall not bear the iniquity of his father and a father shall not bear the iniquity of his son; the righteousness of the righteous person shall be upon him and the wickedness of the wicked person shall be upon him.

As for the wicked man, if he repents from all his sins that he committed, and he observes all My decrees and practices justice and righteousness, he shall surely live, he shall not die. All his transgressions that he committed will not be remembered against him; he shall live because of the righteousness that he did. Do I desire at all the death of the wicked man? - the word of the Lord YHWH/ELOHIM. Is it not rather his return from his ways, that he might live?

And when a righteous man turns away from his righteousness and practices corruption, shall he do like all the abominations that the wicked man did, and live? All his righteousness that he had done will not be remembered because of his treachery with which he betrayed and because of his sin that he sinned. Because of them, he shall die!

And if you should say, 'The way of my Lord is not proper' - hear now, O House of Israel! Is My way not proper? Surely it is your ways that are not proper! When the righteous man turns away from his righteousness and practices corruption, he shall die for them; for the corruption that he practiced he shall die. And <u>if the wicked man turns away from his wickedness that he did and performs justice and righteousness, he will cause his soul to live. Because he contemplated and repented from all his transgressions that he did he shall surely live; he shall not die.</u> Yet the House of Israel says, 'The way of my Lord is not proper.' Are My ways not proper, O House of Israel? Surely it is your ways that are not proper! <u>Therefore, I will judge you, each man according to his ways, O House of Israel - the word of the Lord HASHEM/ELOHIM. Turn yourselves back and live!"</u>

***"performs justice and righteousness" would be repentance and restitution as told by God in the Torah, which preceded when God said: "And so he shall be forgiven."

All the words of God are reasonable, just, dependable, and true; He will be faithful to uphold His word as given - but not the altered words, and certainly not the promises or teachings of corrupted men (Those who uphold the "oral torahs"). or a false apostle. His faithfulness will be to uphold those who trust His Instructions to be their manner of life and conduct. The fact is that God does not desire anyone perish, but has declared who loves Him, as well as who He deems cursed and wicked. Considering that God is the same yesterday, today and forever - and that He will uphold His word - those who believe the love of God is unconditional had best repent and go to both the Ten Decrees from Mount Sinai, as well as the "The Blessings and the Curses" to see what Elohim really said and know that He has not altered His word. No doubt false prophets and false accusers (satans) have tried to alter His word in an attempt to prevent us from knowing and believing it. It is also likely Paul was foisted up to get us to believe in the "Church State" that those who fled to the New World sought to escape!!! Open both of your eyes - open both of your ears - open your mind to the words of God:

Printed in the USA
CPSIA information can be obtained
at www.ICGtesting.com
CBHW060101191024
16045CB00039B/1444